written and illustrated
by
Judy Mulford

Library of Congress Catalog Card Number:
86-90442

Second printing 1988
Third printing 1991

All photographs by author unless otherwise credited.

To my family:
With love to
Mommy and Daddy and Ed
Lei-Ann and Andy
Lauren and Bill
and especially..
most especially,
with all my heart..
to
Danny

TABLE OF CONTENTS

~ Introduction ~

There is something magical about pine needle basketry. Every needle becomes an important individual as it is carefully collected, sorted, washed and dried and then lovingly added to a basket.

A pine needle basket is a very personal statement and so is this book. The book is small so it will fit into your purse, pocket or backpack. I have hand lettered the book because I wanted to put down each letter as carefully as I pick up each pine needle.

Enjoy ~ Judy

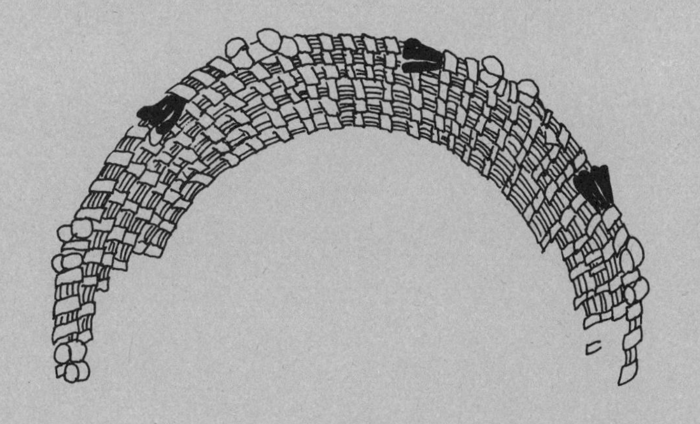

history

2

HISTORY

Basketry, one of the oldest crafts, dates back some 9,000 years. The American Indians used over one hundred different natural materials and the area in which they lived determined the materials available for use in their baskets.

Historical references do not indicate a wide use of pine needles in the basketry of the American Indian. However, because of the availability of pine needles, the Seminole Indians of South Florida are thought to be the first pine needle basket makers. The needles were used in bundles and were sewn together with fern roots, swamp grass and sisal using a bone or shell needle or awl.

Modern day use of pine needles in basketry may have begun during the Civil War times (1861-1865) when Mrs. M. J Mac Afee of Southern Georgia used pine needles bound together with cotton thread to replace a worn hat for her father. She claimed to be the originator of pine needle basketry as we know it today, but others have also laid claim to this distinction.

Raffia, from the Raffia Palm in Madagascar, soon replaced cotton thread as a binder and women, following the Civil War, began making pine needle baskets, trays, purses, pin cushions, hats, desk caddies and lamp shades. Classes were taught, several "how to" books were written, (See Bibliography) and the distinct American pine needle basketry form was on its way.

ca 1920 - origin unknown.
Pine needles and raffia in
natural, red, yellow and
black. Diameter = 7 inches,
height (with lid) = 5 inches.

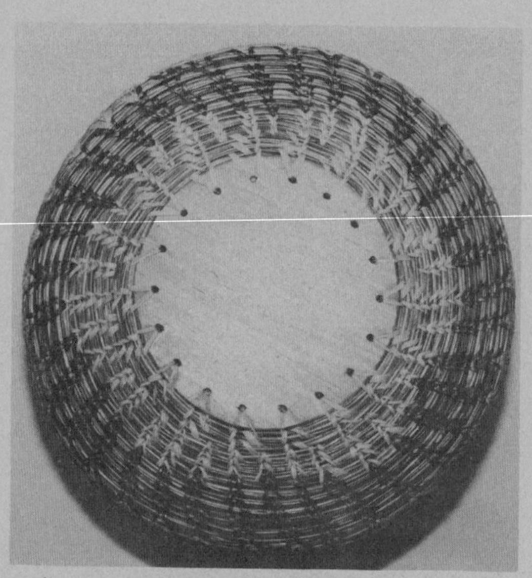

Wooden bottom. Colors more
vivid on the bottom and inside.

ca 1930, Tennessee; pine needles and raffia; teneriffe designs; length-9½ inches, width-5¼ inches, height-7 inches; collected by Ruth Ozanich.

Today several North American Indian groups are using pine needles in their basketry. The Coushatta, or Koasati, Indians (originally from North Central Alabama) have lived in Louisiana since the late 1700's. Many live in the small community of Elton, west of Lafayette, and are now producing many pine needle baskets. Their close neighbors, the Alibamu and the Chitimacha, also produce similar baskets.

In the 1920's, sedge grass for basket use was hard to obtain, so the Coushattas switched to using the abundant Longleaf Pine (Pinus palustris). Raffia, used at that time to tie bundles of onions in the local markets, was used as a binder.

Coushatta - 1985; pine needles, raffia (natural and black); diameter ~ 4½ inches; height ~ 2¾ inches.

Coushatta - 1985; pine needles, raffia (natural and red and green); diameter ~ 4½ inches, height - 3¼ inches.

Coushatta - 1985; pine needles, raffia (natural, purple, red); length - 4 3/4 inches, width - 4 inches, height - 3 inches.

Today the Coushattas are almost exclusively producing pine needle baskets. The basket shapes range from small round or oval baskets with tight fitting lids to larger baskets and effigy baskets shaped like frogs, turkeys, owls, alligators and others.

Some baskets have colored raffia designs of flowers stitched onto their lids or sides while others are embellished with pine cone scales, mussel shell disks and beads.

The use of natural dyes among the Coushattas is minimal. Commercial dyes are preferred along with colors obtained by boiling crepe paper. The Alibamu tend to be more conservative than the Coushattas with their color use.

Because of the popularity of these pine needle baskets, this technique is spreading throughout the western southeast into the Cherokee, Yuchi and Choctow tribes.

Gullah - 1985; pine needles, bull rush, palmetto palm; diameter - 8 inches, height - 2¼ inches.

The Gullah-Afro Americans of Mt. Pleasant, South Carolina also produce large quantities of pine needle baskets. They are descendants of negro slaves brought to America from Africa and they now reside in a small area just north of Charleston and on the Sea Islands off the coast. Their basket techniques are identical to the coil baskets made on the West Coast of Africa except that the Gullahs have introduced the longleaf pine needles as a decorative element.

Traditionally, the Gullahs made coiled "fanner" baskets to clean grain (first documented in 1730). These were made with rush and bound with palmetto butt or white oak. Today the core is made with sweet grass, bull rush and longleaf pine needles (called "pine straw") and bound with palmetto palm strips.

At the turn of this century, work basket production for agricultural and household use changed to include more decorative or "show" baskets. The Gullah basketry techniques have been handed down from mother to daughter until now over 60 family operated stands are along a stretch of U.S. Highway 17 north of Charleston.

Gullah - 1985; pine needles, sweet grass, bull rush, palmetto palm; diameter - 9 inches, height - 3 inches.

The coiled baskets are made in a clockwise direction using a knotted beginning of pine needles or sweet grass (Sporobulus gracilis). An awl, made from a teaspoon broken off at the bowl and the narrow end filed to a wedge point, is used to pierce the bundle so the binder, palmetto palm (Serenoa repens), can be pushed through.

Gullah - 1985

Decorative elements are created by alternating the rows with different fibers and by tying the pliable pine needles into "French knots".

The Seminoles of South Florida share the basketry techniques of the Coushattas and Gullahs. Today sweet grass is almost entirely used as the core, but some weavers use pine needles for designs. They use cotton thread as a binder and the flat bottoms of their baskets are made with cardboard covered with matted palmetto palm fiber.

The Tarahumara Indians of the Sierra Madre Occidental region of northwestern Mexico make small, twill plaited, double walled and nested baskets using long, green needles. These are made to sell to tourists.

Tarahumara - 1982; pine needles; diameter - 5¼ inches, height - 2 inches.
~ Six nested baskets ~

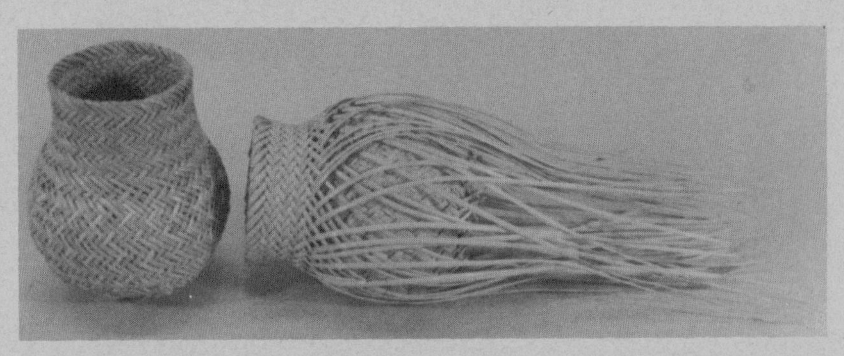

Tarahumara - 1982, double walled basket (left) diameter - 3½ inches, height - 3½ inches; unfinished basket on the right.

On the West Coast, near San Diego, the Diegueño Indians have occasionally made pine needle baskets using Coulter Pine needles (Pinus coulteri) with a sumac start and juncus

(*Juncus textiles*) as a binder. Other North American Indian groups also occasionally used pine needles in their basketry, but it is not well documented.

Luiseno, ca 1940, S. California; Torrey and other pine needles, raffia, diameter - 8¼ inches, height - 6 inches.

Cahuilla, pre 1956, S. California; pine needles, raffia; diameter - 7 inches. height - 3 inches.

Paiute, ca 1900, Coulter pine needles, raffia, bark bottom; diameter - 7 inches. height - 2½ inches.

Baskets on this page are from the Natural History Museum of Los Angeles County.

materials
3

~MATERIALS~

NECESSARY SUPPLIES:

1. Pine needles (of course!)
2. Sewing materials
3. Sewing needles
4. Scissors
5. Blunt table knife
6. Towel and plastic bag

OPTIONAL SUPPLIES:

7. Gauge
8. Thimbles
9. Rings/wire
10. Shellac and denatured alcohol.

I. PINE NEEDLES:

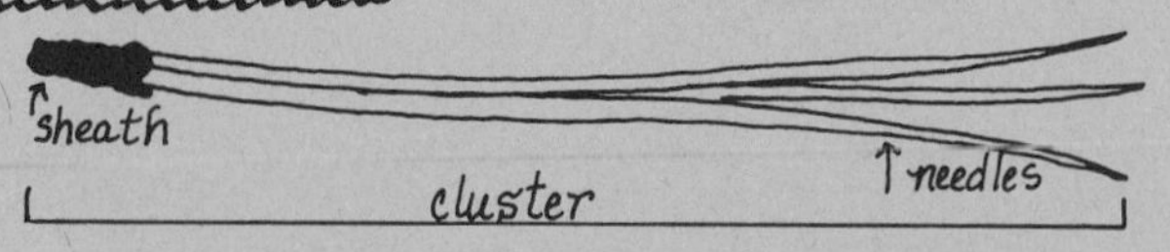

Pine needle basketry is a total life experience. You don't just "make" a basket with pine needles, you have to gather your materials before you even begin. This may be a simple task of going out into your own yard or a neighbors', or, taking a full day to go up into the mountains or to an area where suitable materials can be gathered. But, wherever you collect, you will find the collecting experience an enjoyable one because you will be outside and in touch with nature ~ and ~ yourself. ~

In many parts of the country you can gather needles at any time of the year as they fall from the trees. But, if you want to collect at higher elevations where it snows, the best time to collect is in late summer or early fall.

Gather the top layer of brown needles that have just fallen from the tree. Needles that have been on the ground too long will be brittle and, sometimes, mildewed due to exposure to sun and rain. You can also pluck the brown needles from the branches before they have fallen from the tree. These tend to be the most pliable.

To collect green needles, take them from a fallen branch or one that has been trimmed. The green needles need to be dried because if they are used green they will shrink when they dry and your basket will be loose.

To dry (or cure) green needles you must dry them in or out of doors for 2 or 3 weeks. If you want a brown color, dry them in the sun on your patio or on a screen and turn them every few days to get an even color. If you would like to retain some of the green color, dry them in the shade away from the sun. If the needles are still on the branches, you can hang them to dry by the branch ends.

You may also dry them in your microwave, but this makes them brittle. To do this, lay your green needles on a paper towel and cover with another paper towel. Microwave on high setting for 2 to 4 minutes opening the door every minute to let out the moisture. This procedure is good to use when you are experimenting with dyeing brown needles and you want to see (right away!) what the true color will be.

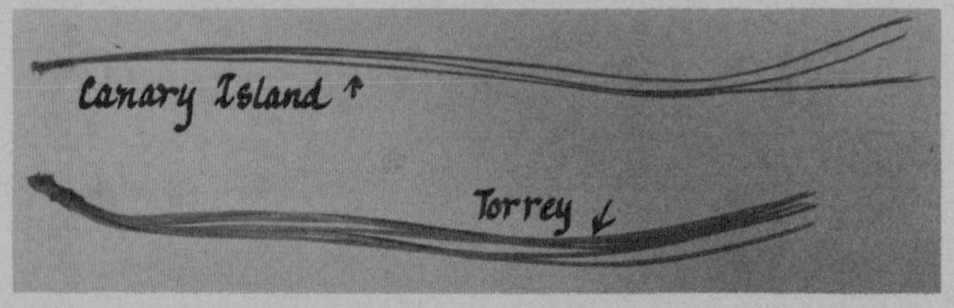

There are many different types of needles that you can use in your basket. Some needles, like the Canary Island, are long and delicate with tiny sheath ends and require many clusters to form a bundle. Others, like the Torrey, are thick and long and have a big sheath and so fewer needles are needed. The needles you use will depend on the look and feel and design that you want in your basket. Remember, you may use several kinds of needles in your basket. The longer the needles you use; the easier it is, but don't forget the shorter ones. These can be used for design elements where longer needles may have to be cut down.

For a list of needles used in pine needle basketry refer to the section on trees on page 127.

If you are collecting large amounts of needles for classes, collect them in large, plastic trash bags. When you get home, remove the needles from the bags and lay them flat in an open box so that air can get to them. If they are kept in a closed plastic bag, moisture can accumulate and the needles will become damp and mildew.

1. Montezuma
2. Torrey
3. Jeffrey
4. Canary Is.

STORING NEEDLES

If you are collecting in smaller amounts, and have the time, just collect the really perfect needles. Arrange them in bundles with the sheath ends pointing in one direction and secure both ends with rubber bands, raffia or string. Or, store them flat in a box. You can wash them later.

WASHING: Before you use your needles, it is best to wash and rinse them to remove the dirt and any small insects that might be present. (If "bugs are eating a finished basket, put it in your freezer for a few days.)

Put one teaspoon or more of any good detergent into one gallon of cold or warm water. Gently agitate the needles in the water to dislodge the dirt. Then rinse them thoroughly to remove the soap. If you are not going to use them right away, dry them, reassemble them in bundles and store.

You may sort the needles before or after you wash them. This means selecting only the whole, unbroken needles and putting them in bundles according to length and type.

SOAKING: If you are ready to start a basket after you have washed your needles, you will need to soak them to make them pliable for the beginning of your basket.

A pliable (flexible) needle that does not need to be soaked is one that can fold over your finger or can be tied in a knot without breaking →

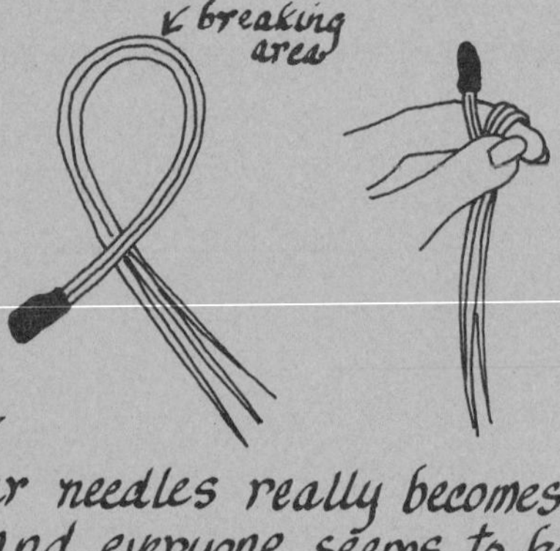

breaking area

Soaking time for your needles really becomes an individual judgement and everyone seems to have their own way for their own particular needles. Some needles are very flexible and need very little or no soaking. Some are very dry and stiff and require more soaking. Following are a few suggestions that you can try to see which method best suits you and your needles: ~

REMEMBER: soaked needles are ONLY used for the beginning 1 to 2 inches in diameter of the basket and in areas where small or sharp turns are required. If you over soak your needles or use only soaked needles for the entire basket, the needles will shrink causing the stitching to become loose and the basket won't be sturdy or firm.

1. Soak clean needles for one hour in cold water or ½ hour in hot water. Remove, wrap in a towel and store in a plastic bag several hours or over night to "mellow". This will permit the moisture to penetrate evenly. The needles may be kept for several days in the plastic bag, but if they are left too long, and it is warm, they may mildew. To retard the mildewing, put the bag of needles in the refrigerator. One Gullah woman said that she put her soaked bag of needles in the freezer to keep.

2. Pour boiling water over the needles and let them sit for 10 to 15 minutes. This will also darken the needles.

3. Wrap dry needles in a very wet towel and store several hours or over night. The needles need to lay flat, not bunched up, on the towel so that the moisture will be evenly accepted.

4. Use one part glycerine (purchased at drug stores) to two parts water and soak for several hours. Glycerine may attract bugs.

If you don't use all of your soaked needles, you may dry them and use them again later.

If you wish to dye your needles, you would dye them after they have been soaked. (see "Dyes", page 115).

SEWING MATERIALS:

You will need some kind of binding material to sew one bundle (coil) of needles to the other. You may use anything you want. Here are a few examples:

- fiber samples →

• SYNTHETIC FIBERS:

1.) Swistraw (viscose rayon ribbon);-made in Switerland; durable, soil and fade resistant; comes in many brilliant and matte finishes.

2.) Poly-Cord-made in China; comes in several colors.

3.) Polyester threads

4.) Monofilament (fishing line) - comes in several weights; clear; can be used where you don't want binding to show.

5.) Yarns - rayon, rayon, etc. or blends that are strong and firm and do not stretch.

• NATURAL FIBERS:

1.) Yarns/strings/threads - in cotton, wool or silk (or blends) that are firm and strong and do not stretch (ex: embroidery thread, crochet cotton, pearl cotton. these may be unraveled for thinner pieces or plied for heavier strands.

2.) Waxed linen - comes in a variety of colors and weights (3,4,6,8,9 and 12 cord - 3 being the lightest.) The heavier weight cords can be divided into lighter weight sewing threads by unraveling the threads. Other fibers can be waxed by pulling them through a piece of beeswax. This will enable the fiber to flow through the bundle more easily and will help prevent fraying.

3.) Plant fibers - dracaena, yucca, flax and other materials can be stripped down and used as a binder.

RAFFIA (raffia will be used in describing the construction of the "basic basket")

Raffia (Raphia ruffia) is a natural fiber that comes from the raffia palm that grows in Madagascar, an island off the East Coast of Africa (Malagasy REPUBLIC). The immense young pinnate palm leaves (fronds) are cut green and the outer, transparent skin is pulled off and hung to air dry in the sun. It is then stripped and graded into fourteen different categories and exported.

~RAFFIA~

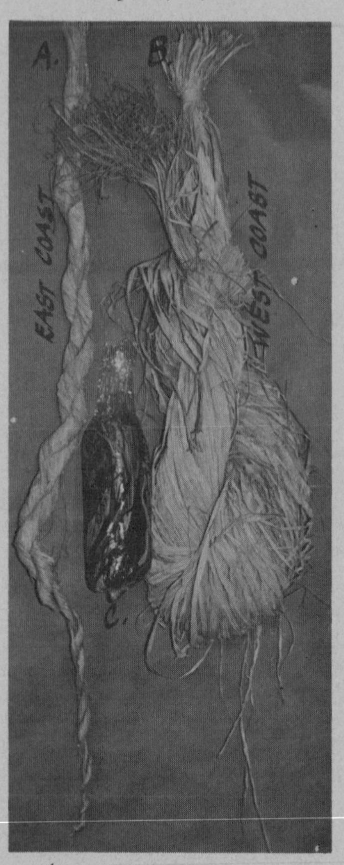

There are two types of raffia - East Coast (A) and West Coast (B). The unprocessed West Coast raffia comes in open type hanks and has a braider and longer leaf. The processed West Coast raffia is dyed, fireproofed and wrapped in cellophane (C.) It comes in a variety of colors, but is not very good for basketry because it shreds, breaks and the colors can come off on your hands. If you are determined to use the treated raffia, remove it from the cellophane bag and air dry it. The raffia tends to sweat in the bag which can further weaken the fibers.

The natural, undyed and unprocessed raffia from the East Coast (A) is the best for use in pine needle basketry. It comes in tightly twisted hanks or "pigtails". To use it, cut off the bottom knot, dip the hank in warm water for 15 to 20 minutes, untwist the fibers and hang it to dry so the leaves will untwist and open. In the past, some people hung their raffia out doors over night to let the dew open the strands. It was brought indoors before the sun came up.

Raffia may be used wet or dry. First remove the side hairs and split the raffia to the width you want. For smooth raffia, removed the rolled edges from each side and save for future use. (teneriffe designs) To flatten the center section, pass a moistened strand between your thumb and fingers or iron it. For an opposite effect, twist the raffia.

If you aren't a perfectionist, just dip a dry strand of raffia into a glass of water (your coffee, tea or wine) for a few seconds and then run the strand through your fingers to expell the excess moisture.

Thread the raffia from the thick or darker stem end. This will help reduce fraying since the leaf grows from the stalk out and the grains of raffia are further apart at the stem end than at the narrow end.

If you have trouble threading the needle on the thick end, thread the thin end and pull the needle to the thick end. Or, fold the raffia over the end of the needle (A) and make a sharp crease. ← Remove the needle and force the creased end (B) through the eye. If you are still having trouble, reduce the width of the raffia or use a needle with a larger eye.

A B

★ TO REDUCE FRAYING: thread thick end; keep raffia damp; don't use wider than 3/4th inch; don't pull on needle end to tighten raffia, pull near basket; change the position of the needle on the raffia while working.

When adding new raffia, use the same width as the previous strand.

3. SEWING NEEDLES:

When you are making your basket, you may use several different sizes of needles depending on the size and shape of your basket. For the beginning student, it is easier to use a needle with a large eye such as a chenille needle in sizes 18, 20 and 22 (sharp points) or a size 18 tapestry needle with a blunt point. The blunt needles are easier to use on the wrapped doughnut beginning and teneriffe designs. The sharp pointed needles work best for the rest of the basket because they pierce the bundle more easily.

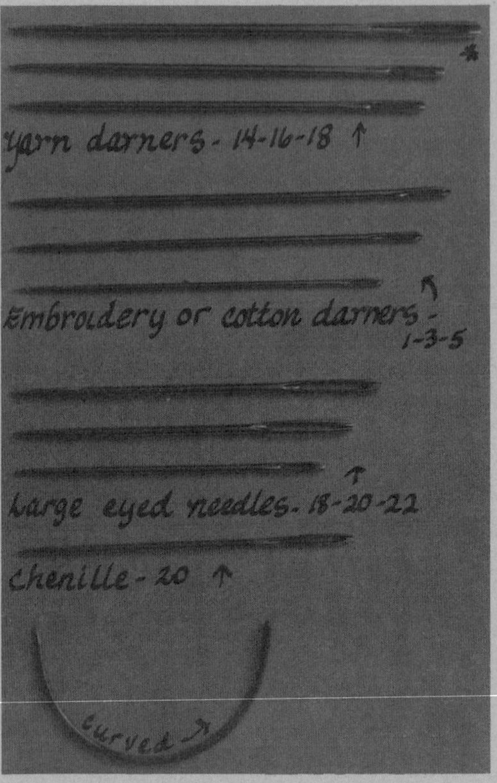

* actual needle size.

The darning needles work the best in most parts of the basket, but you may have to switch to a shorter needle in some tight working areas. A curved needle works well in areas with very narrow openings. It is best to have an assortment of needles.

4. SCISSORS: sharp with a good point (embroidery scissors)

5. BLUNT TABLE KNIFE: used for scrapping the sheath off the cluster. You can also use your thumbnail. Don't use your teeth.

6. TOWEL AND PLASTIC BAG: for storing your moistened pine needles.

OPTIONAL SUPPLIES:

7. GAUGE: Many basket makers use a gauge to control the thickness of their bundle (I do not). This can be a piece of straw or plastic, copper or aluminium tubing 5/8th to 1 inch long by 3/16th to 1/4th inch in diameter -or, any diameter you want. The gauge is fed by removing the sheath from a cluster and inserting it into the gauge on the bundle. Rolling the gauge helps ease the pine needles into place creating a smoother finish. A gauge is not used if the sheath is left on for a decorative effect.

8. THIMBLES: You may use a regular thimble or a Japanese thimble (B) (it looks like a wide, textured ring) Or, you may purchase or make a finger stall that goes over the end of your finger. The stall can be made from a piece of soft leather.

A. finger stall

B. Japanese thimble

9. RINGS/WIRE: used for Teneriffe designs; rings 1/2 inch to 4 inches in diameter are recommended. Metal rings are preferred, but you can use wood

or plastic rings. You can also make your own rings or other shapes with galvanized 16 to 18 gauge wire that has been bent to the desired shape and the ends soldered. You can make your own wire pattern by pounding headless nails into a board, wrapping your wire around the nails and soldering the ends together.

10. SHELLAC: Shellacking stiffens and protects the basket and gives it a shine. You may want to shellac a basket if it is tiny and delicate or if it is loose and wobbly and won't hold its shape. Use only pure, white shellac because others will yellow with age. Get small containers because the shellac will discolor if exposed to the air too often. Use 2 parts shellac to 1 part denatured alcohol. Or, you can use 1 part shellac to 1 part alcohol for the first coat, let dry and give a final coat of shellac and allow to dry 24 hours. Some people wax and polish the basket.

To dry your shellacked basket, dry it on a bed of nails. Put a thin piece of wood on the ground and pound a bunch of nails through to the other side so they protrude ½ inch or more.

Remember - If you use shellac you will be covering up the beautiful pine scent of your needles.

~

4

~WEAVING A BASIC BASKET~

Pine needle baskets are made with the coiling technique which is one of the oldest and most universal methods of basket making. The basket is built by coiling and stitching one continuous bundle around and on top of the row below. The foundation is comprised of a bundle of pine needles bound together with a binding material of raffia, thread or other fibers.

You can easily make a small basket in one day even if you are a beginner. The most successful way is to work on the bottom of the basket in the morning for three hours. After lunch, spend another three hours turning up the sides and completing the basket. This schedule works beautifully in a class situation. Remember, you will only make a small basket in six hours, but there is always a second, larger basket to follow.

Don't be concerned about making a "perfect" basket→ Just MAKE IT!! If you make a "mistake", remember that there really aren't any mistakes- only "adaptations". Don't take out any of the basket unless you absolutely have to. This is ONLY a a basket and if you don't enjoy making it, don't do it!

Please keep your first, sample basket. It is a very special, magical basket and no one will love and appreciate it as much as you do. If you must give it to some one, give it to some one you love that lives with you.

STARTING YOUR BASKET

The beginning of the basket is very important. The many different ways that coiled baskets are started help anthropologists to culturally identify historical pieces. The beginning is also the nucleus of the basket and is often a focal point, so care should be taken with its execution.

Unfortunately, the beginning is also the most difficult part of the basket. It would be much easier to start with the ending and end with the beginning.

IMPORTANT: All of the directions are for the RIGHT HANDED weaver and you will work in a counter clock wise direction, or, from RIGHT to LEFT (left handed weavers reverse directions.)

There are many ways to start a coiled basket, but I will describe only three approaches: the "doughnut", oval and knotted beginnings. The "doughnut" directions begin on the next page. Oval and knotted starts are on page 79.

The Doughnut:

Select a long piece of raffia, dip it in water for a few seconds and pull it between your thumb and fingers to expell the excess water. Thread the thicker or darker end of the strand with a needle. (refer to section on raffia) page 25.

Select 4 to 5 premoistened long pine needle clusters (refer to section on pine needle preparation). These, held together in a bundle, should be a "pencil" thickness. (I do not use a gauge) Think "pencil" thickness and you can use any needles you want. If you are using Torrey Pine needles, you may need 2 clusters; Jeffrey - 5, Canary Island - 10 and so forth. If you want a larger bundle, think "crayola" thickness. Or, if you want a smaller bundle, think smaller. Single needles and not whole clusters may also be used. But, whatever you decide, keep this "Thought Thickness" in your mind and fingers throughout the basket.

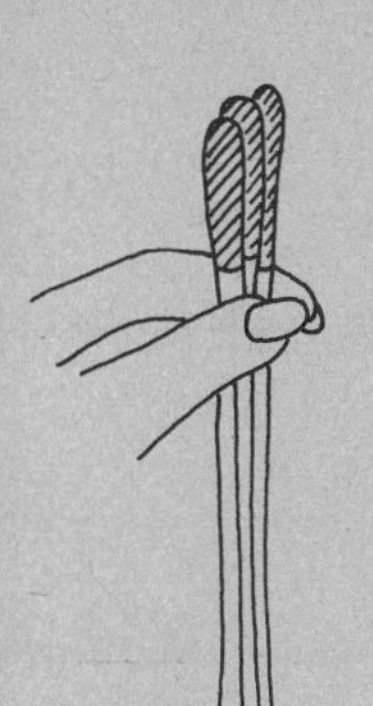

With your left hand, hold a "pencil" thickness cluster of needles between your thumb and forefinger with the sheath ends pointing up. ←

Fold the long ends around your forefinger to form a loop and hold with your thumb. →

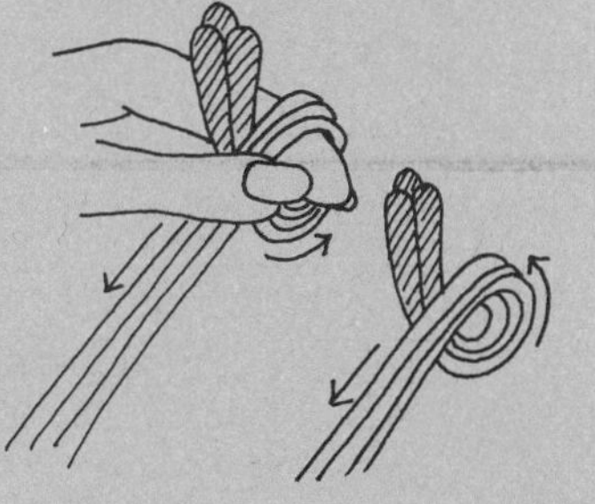

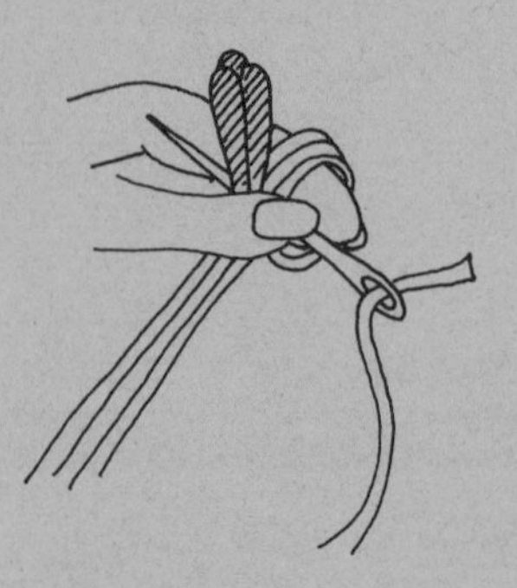

Place the threaded needle under the loop between the needles and your forefinger. ←

Pull the raffia to the narrow end and tie it in a single or double knot. Drop your → needle before tying the knot so you won't poke your eye out. →

We will always be working from the front to the back.

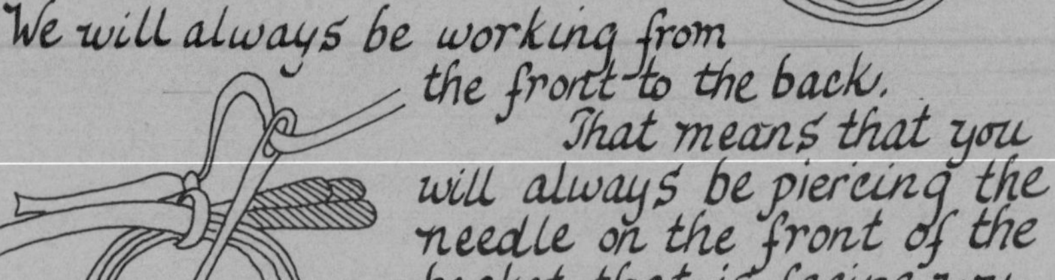

That means that you will always be piercing the needle on the front of the basket that is facing you.

Lay the short end of the knotted raffia along the long ends of the pine needles and hold down with your left hand.

← With your right hand, and moving to the left, wrap around and over the pine needles from front to back.

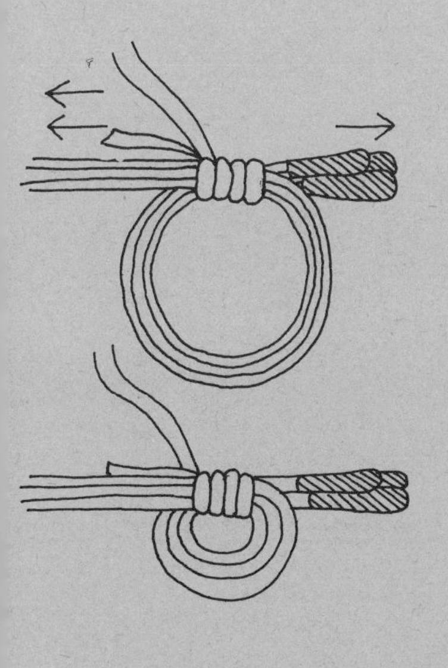

When the needles have been wrapped 4 to 6 times, gently pull on both ends to tighten the circle. Do not pull on the short end of the raffia. Pull more on the long needle ends than on the sheath ends.

If the needles do not pull evenly into a tight circle, carefully pull each needle end until the problem is corrected.

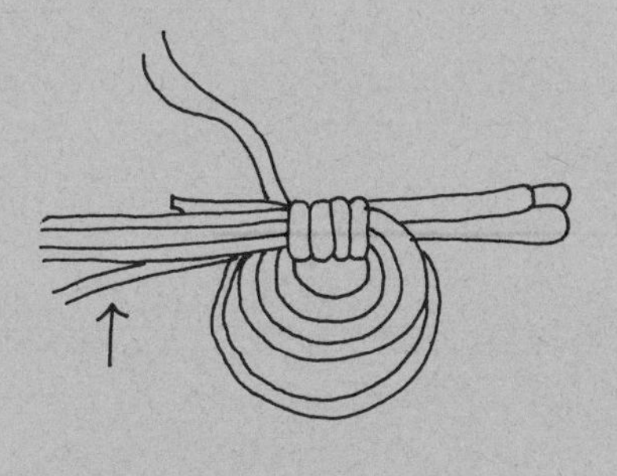

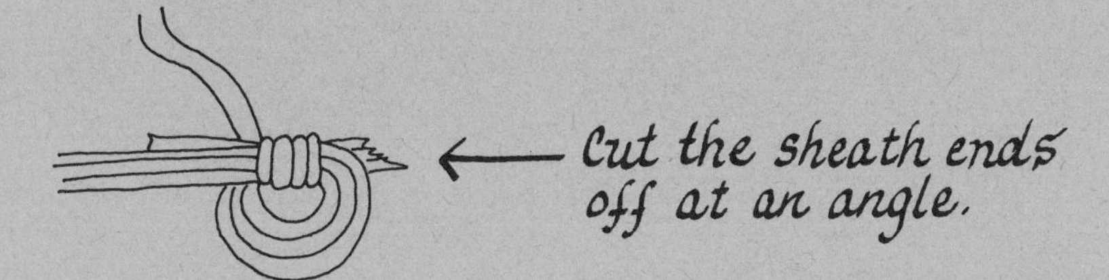

Cut the sheath ends off at an angle.

Continue wrapping around the doughnut catching in the tapered ends. Keep the raffia smooth and flat. If the raffia bunches up or overlaps too much it will be difficult to pierce the doughnut with a needle.

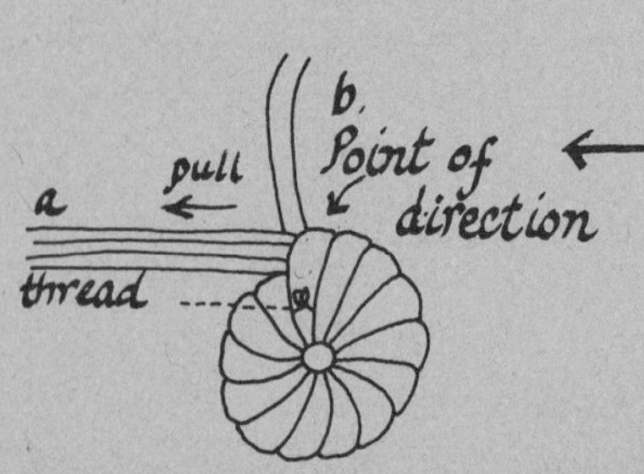

When the doughnut is completely covered, hold it with the thumb and forefinger of your right hand and pull on the loose ends (a) to tighten. This last LONG stitch that has formed is very important.

It is called the POINT OF DIRECTION, MOVEMENT or BEGINNING - and you will refer to it many times. Mark this long stitch (b) with a thread or pen.

Point of Direction

✡ It is from this point that all stitch and color changes are made, the shaping changes occur and where the basket is ended. Follow the POINT OF DIRECTION stitch straight up. Do not follow the spiral line of the stitch.

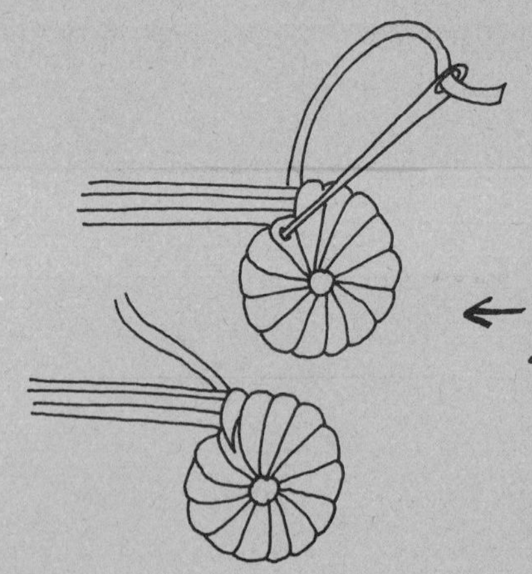

STOP STITCH or "BOING" STITCH

To secure your doughnut's wrapping, you must take a stop stitch 1/3 way down into the doughnut or your wrapping will loosen and "boing" out. This is a good place to stop and prepare your needles for your core (bundle) if you have not already done so. If you don't start adding to your core at this time, your needles will run out and you will be finished before you really start...

If the doughnut raffia is too wide, it will make heavy, thick stitches. Split it as this time and cut off the excess. Narrow raffia can be used near the center and can be increased in width as the basket progresses and the stitches get further apart.

ADDING RAFFIA - "THE EASIEST" WAY →

If you run out of raffia on the doughnut or anywhere else, the easiest way to attach a new piece is to tie (square knot) it to the old piece. Make sure that the knot sits squarely on top of the row so it will be hidden when the next row goes on top of it. This may take some practice. For other ways of ending and adding raffia refer to page 73.

ADDING TO THE BUNDLE

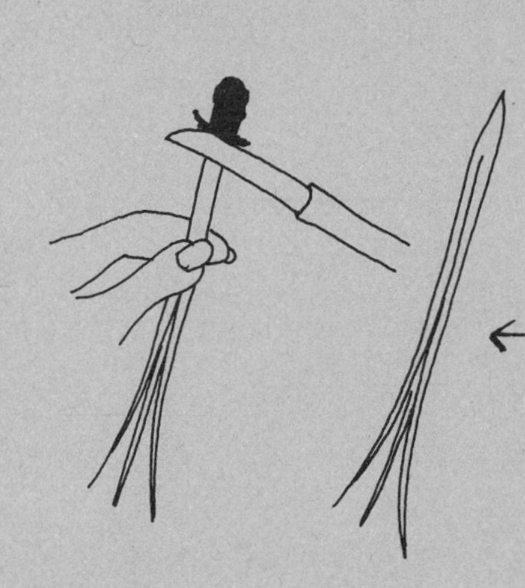

To remove the sheath ends from a cluster of needles, gently scrape the ends off with a table knife or with your thumb nail. If you are careful, the cluster will remain in tact and not fall apart.

Prepare about 20 or 30 clusters and keep them damp in a towel.

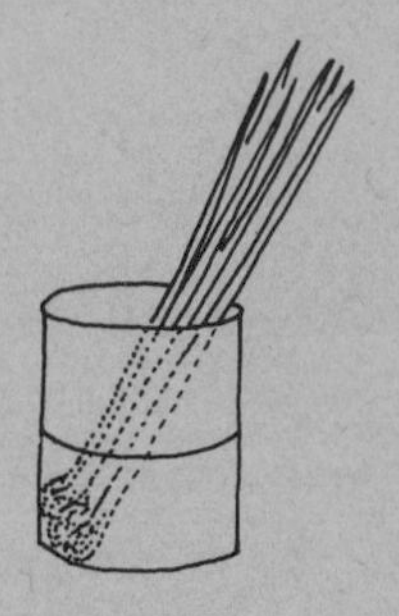

If you are working with unmoistened needles and the sheaths are difficult to remove, set the tips in a glass of water for a few minutes to soften them.

If all of the bundle needles end in the same place forming a blunt end, taper the needles.

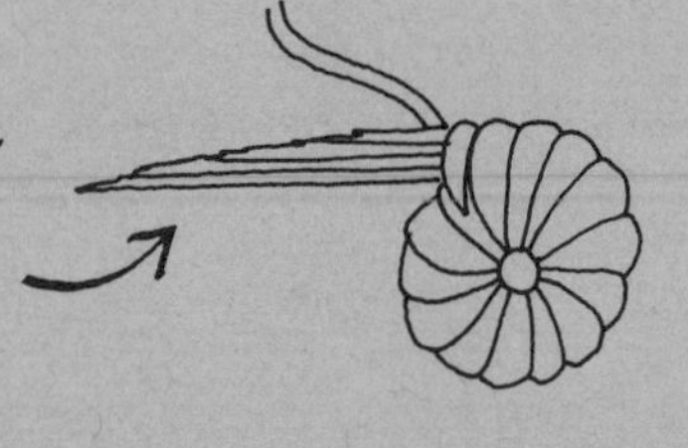

Slip a sheathless cluster of needles into the middle or bottom of the bundle and under the last stitch. For the first row you may have to add clusters every few stitches to build up and maintain the size of bundle that you want. There is no exact rule as to how many needles are added and how often they are added. Each basket is different. It takes practice to be able to maintain an even bundle.

THE FIRST ROW:

The first row of stitches is very important. They must be placed evenly around the doughnut so that a nice, evenly spaced spiral will form as the basket progresses. You may place the stitches close together so they cover the bundle or you may space them to expose the needles. ↗

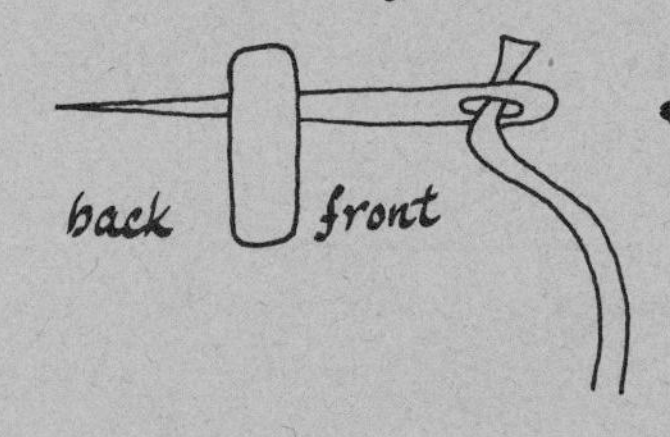

← Place the needle from front to back straight through the top third of the bundle. You may need pliers to pull the needle through the dough-nut.

Keep this row directly on top of the doughnut edge. Continue going around in a circle making stitches and → feeding the bundle until you get to the "point of direction".

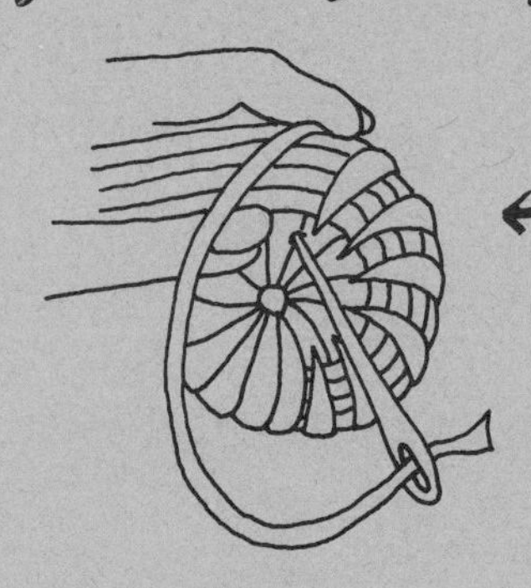

← It is important that your stitches are tight so your basket will be firm. Pull the raffia near the basket and not at the needle end. Hold the raffia taut with your left finger. on top of the bundle.

SECOND ROW:

For a basic basket, there are two easy stitches that you can do - the "straight stitch" and the "split stitch" (For more stitches see page 55).

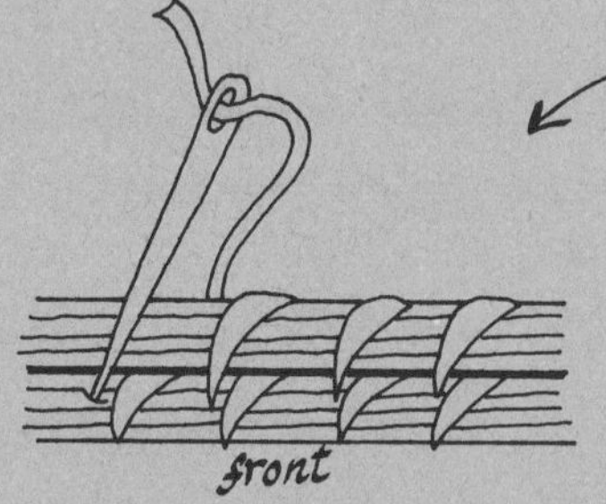

STRAIGHT STITCH (also called whip, plain and rope stitch.)

Insert the needle from front to back to the left of the stitch and about 1/2 down in the bundle.

Push the needle straight → through the bundle. When you work from the front to the back, you have more control over your stitches. Do not try to split the stitch on the back side. A different pattern will form on the other side.

back front

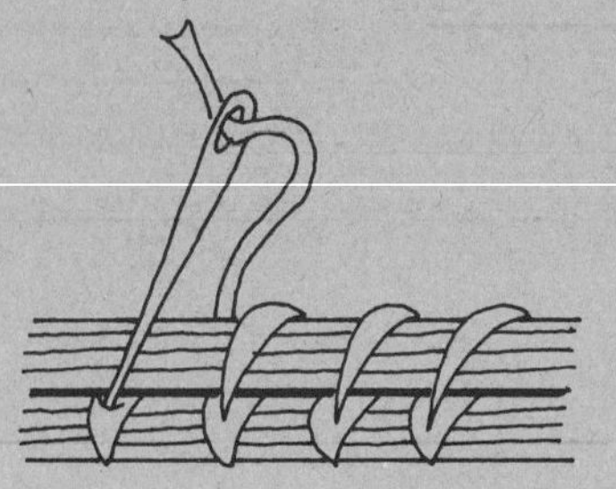

SPLIT STITCH (chain)

Insert the needle through the center of the stitch below.

Spiral effect created when using the above stitches. →

ADDING RAFFIA:

You will, of course, need to add new lengths of binding material. You may just knot a new piece onto the old as previously described, or you may end and add your binder in many different ways. It depends on what material you are using and what part of the basket you are working on. The following description works well on flat areas. For other approaches see page 71. OR, make up you own way...

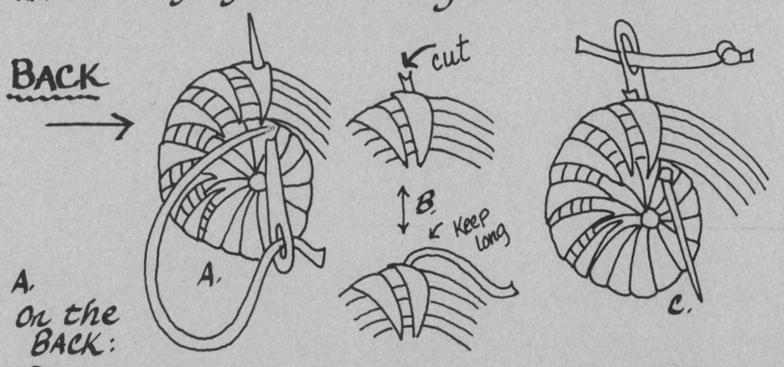

A. On the BACK:

Take a small scooped stitch under the hole where your needle just came out. Push the needle up through the bundle into the last stitch and cut it off or leave it long and push it into the bundle or carry it along the top. (B) To add another length (C), knot another strand, pierce the needle on top of the last stitch, push it down through the bundle into the row below and come out where your "Scoop" stitch was taken.

The knot will sit on top of the bundle and will be hidden by the next row - (D). If you don't want a knot, keep a long end and twist it with the old (E) strand and push into the bundle.

D. FRONT

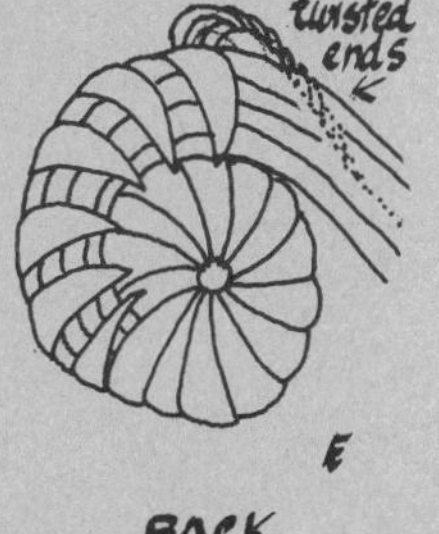

On the last row of your basket, pull the knot into the center of the bundle so it won't show. This can be done throughout the basket.

Continue with these stitches for the remainder of the three hours (or, for a larger bottom, work as long as you want...)

If the stitches get too far apart (½ inch), add another stitch inbetween each stitch — or, add them just where they are needed.

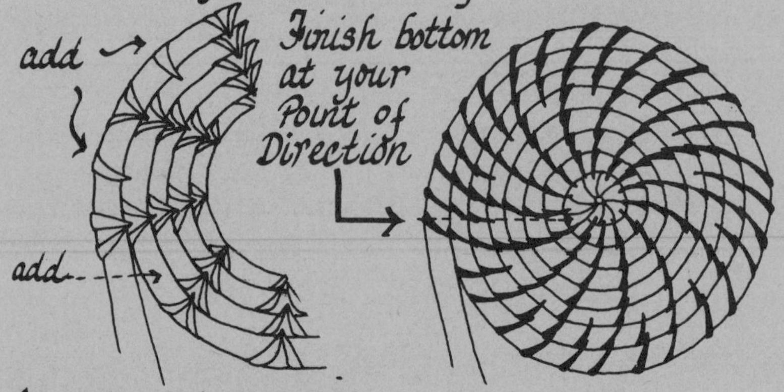

ADDING NEW STITCHES:

~ Shaping Your Basket ~

When you finish making the bottom of your basket, it is time to shape the sides. If you have spent the morning three hours working on the bottom, you will spend three hours in the afternoon shaping and completing your basket.

Before you begin to shape the sides, recheck to make sure that you have stopped at your Point of Direction.

There is a RIGHT (front) SIDE and a WRONG (back) SIDE to the basket. The RIGHT SIDE is the side you work on and that faces you.

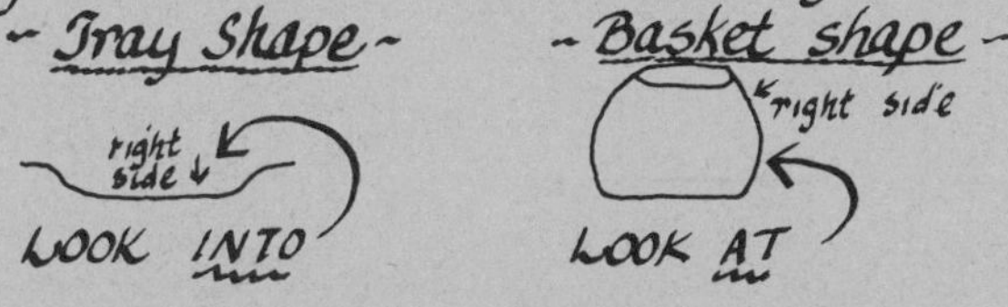

There are two ways to shape your basket: You may make a flat TRAY SHAPE that you look INTO or you can make a closed BASKET SHAPE that you look AT.

TRAY SHAPE:

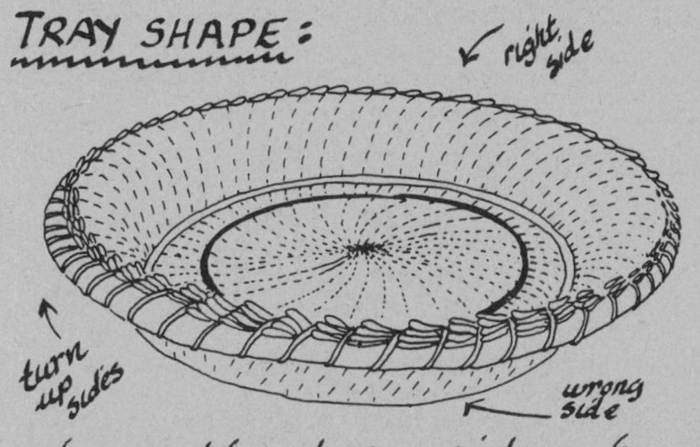

If you want a tray shape, you will want the right side on the face of the tray that you look down into. This means that you will shape the tray sides by turning or flaring the sides (bundles) in toward the right side and toward yourself. The wrong side will be the bottom. (See drawing on next page ... →)

Tray bottom with bundle turning in TOWARD the "right" side and TOWARD yourself. The needle will angle up at this point.

BASKET SHAPE:

If you want a basket shape, you will want the right side on the outside of the basket and the wrong side on the inside of the basket where it will not show. This means that you will shape the basket by having the right side on the bottom of the basket and you will turn the sides AWAY from the right side and AWAY from yourself. Your needle will angle up.

right side

We will be making a basket shape, but if you want to make a tray, just reverse the angle of the bundle.

wrong side

STRAIGHT SIDES

right side on bottom

Before you begin shaping your basket, decide what kind of a shape you want:

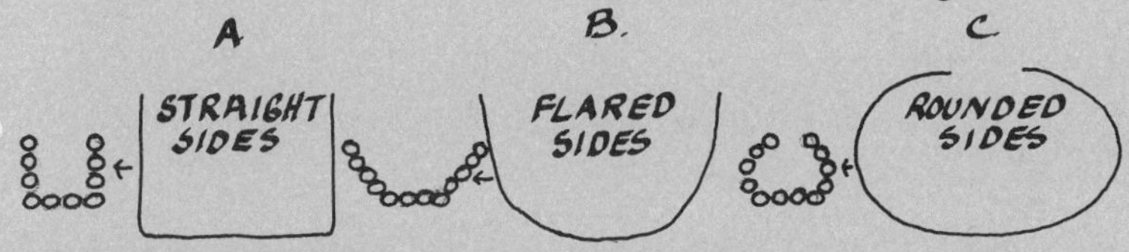

A — STRAIGHT SIDES

B. — FLARED SIDES

C — ROUNDED SIDES

STRAIGHT SIDES:

If you want abrupt straight sides (A), you must place your bundle directly on top of the last row. (See drawing on preceding ← page). Your needle will not be going straight through the bundle for this row but will be going at an angle with the needle pointing up.

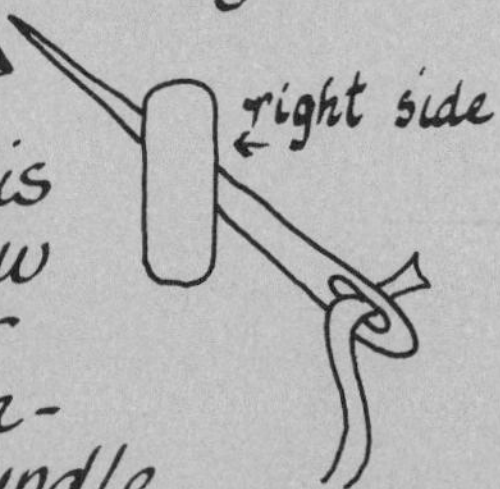

right side

You will continue with your needle at this angle for the first row until you reach your Point of Direction. Continue to "feed" your bundle.

The next row will sit directly on top of the last row as it did on the disk bottom. and the needle will go back to going straight through the bundle.

2nd

mid

bottom

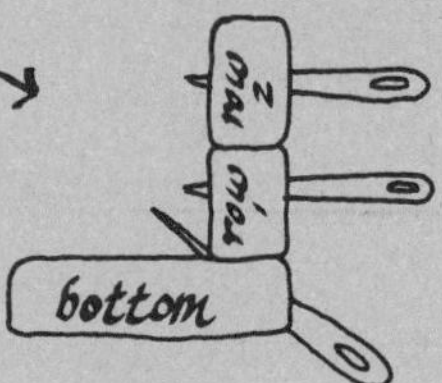

It is easier to work straight up with the basket sitting on a table.

FLARED AND ROUNDED SIDES:

If you want the sides to flare out (B) or have a closed, rounded shape (C), place the bundle at a slight angle to the last row on the outside of the basket. Your needle will be going at a sharp angle with

right side

the tip pointing up. Continue with this same angle for one row. On the next row, place the bundle up a little higher on the previous row. The way you place your bundle is the way you shape your basket.

A. B. C.

As the angle of your bundle changes, so does your needle angle. When you are flaring out (A.), your needle points up. When your sides are flaring in (B), your needle points down toward the inside of the basket.

It is comfortable to work with the basket on your knee or in your lap.

In a class situation, I usually have the students flare the sides out for 1½ hours, go straight up for another half hour or 45 minutes and then flare in and finish off the basket for the remaining time.

FINISHING:

When you are on the last row and are 2½ to 3 inches from your Point of Direction (where your basket should "officially" end), set the basket on a table and squat down so your eyes are level with the rim. Turn the basket slowly around "eye balling" the rim to see where the coil starts to go up. Put a pin in at this point. Sometimes, especially with beginners, the coil may turn up before or beyond the Point of Direction.

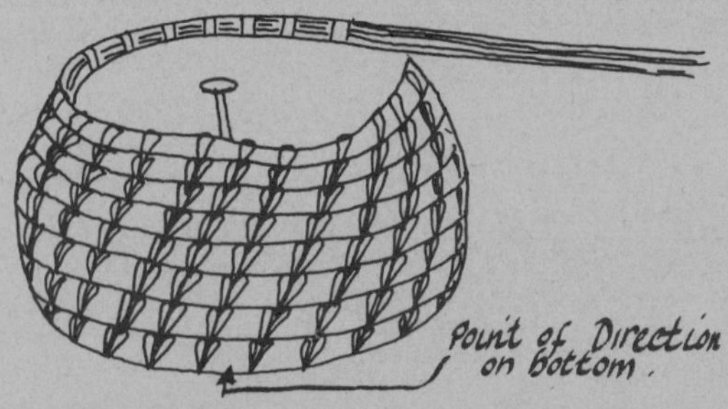

Blunt cut your needles at this point.

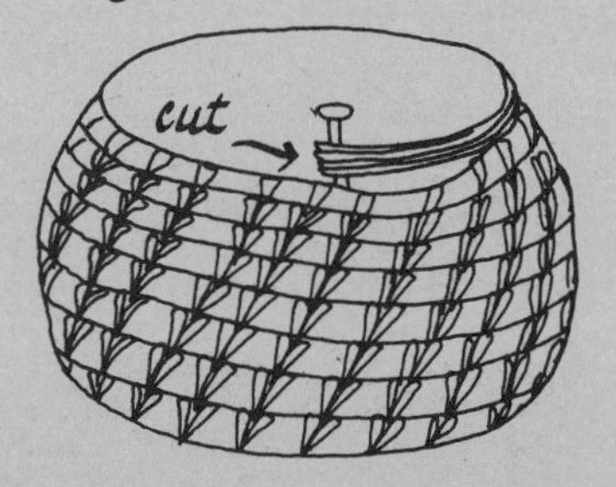

Cut the needles off at an angle on the underside of the bundle and continue stitching to the end. DO NOT continue to feed the bundle or you will never end!

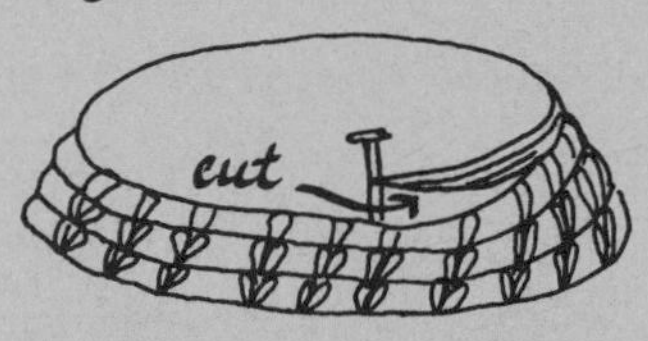

On the last few stitches, go into the stitches on the row below. End off your raffia.

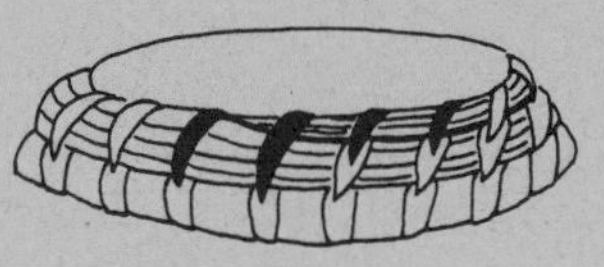

CROSSED STITCH-EDGE:

Before ending your raffia, go backwards (to the right)→ into the base of each stitch. This helps to strengthen the edge and to hold in loose ends.

WRAPPED EDGE:

You can also wrap the edge with raffia. Pierce the needle into the row below or place between the coils and wrap around the bundle.

SHEATH DESIGNS:

If you are using pine needles, you might as well use the beautiful sheaths as part of the design in your basket. Once you have figured out how many you want to use and where you want to place them, it is much easier and faster than constantly feeding the bundle.

Each basket design decision is different because it depends on the needles you use, the size of your bundle and how far apart your stitches are. If you can plan ahead... try to remember how many needles you put into your bundle and how often you put them in. This can help you with your sheath design.

Spiral designs:

Count your stitches to see if you have an odd or an even number. If you have 40 stitches and have been adding one cluster to your bundle every stitch, you can add two sheathed clusters every two stitches or four clusters every fourth stitch. If you have an odd number and want an even number, add another stitch on the first row in a wide space or eliminate a closely spaced stitch.

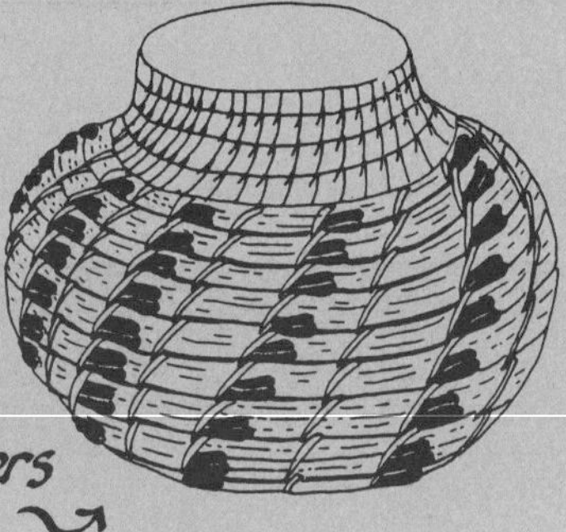

If you have an odd number and place a sheath every other stitch, you will create a more angled spiral or a checker board pattern.

Your design is determined by your sheath placement, the type of needle you use and how many sheath clusters are used. For this first row you need to do a little experimenting.

Make sure to place the sheath close to the bottom of the bundle. If they are up too high on the bundle, the next row will be forced up higher than you want.

If the sheaths stick out too far, they will break off more easily.

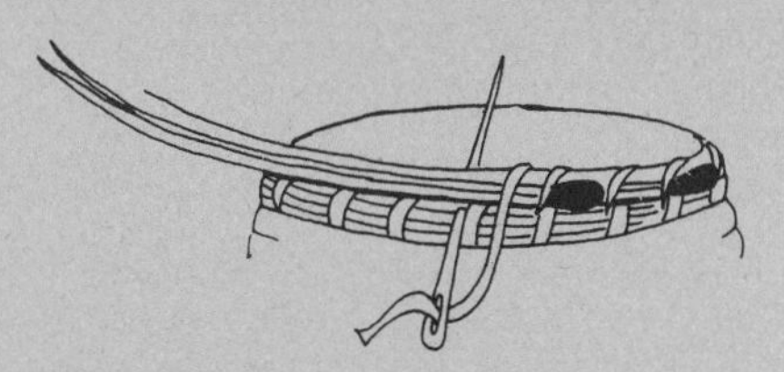

MAINTAINING BUNDLE SIZE:

When you are designing with sheaths, you have to take your bundle size into consideration. You can't say: "I want 10 sheaths showing every stitch", because your bundle will build up and be HUGE!

If you must use a certain amount of needles for your designing needs and the bundle builds up, you can reduce the bundle in several ways:

1. thin the bundle by cutting some of the inner bundle needles.
2. cut the needles (before using them) to make them shorter.
3. Remove a needle from the cluster
4. Use shorter needles.

If you are using only a few sheaths for your design and your bundle is thinning out, add to the bundle like you did on the bottom disk.

Once you have established your sheath pattern and have control over your bundle size, the basket will progress quickly.

You may want the sheaths showing on only parts of your basket. Use your imagination. For your first basket it is best to keep the design simple. You can always experiment on future baskets as you become more secure with your techniques.

Pine needles, raffia.

8" - wide
18" - high

← split stitch

← wrapped

← wheat stitch

M.

J.M.

Pine needles, raffia; split stitch;
8" wide x 6" high

JM

"Quail Basket", - pine needles, raffia,
split stitch, wrapped rim on top.
9" wide x 8" high.

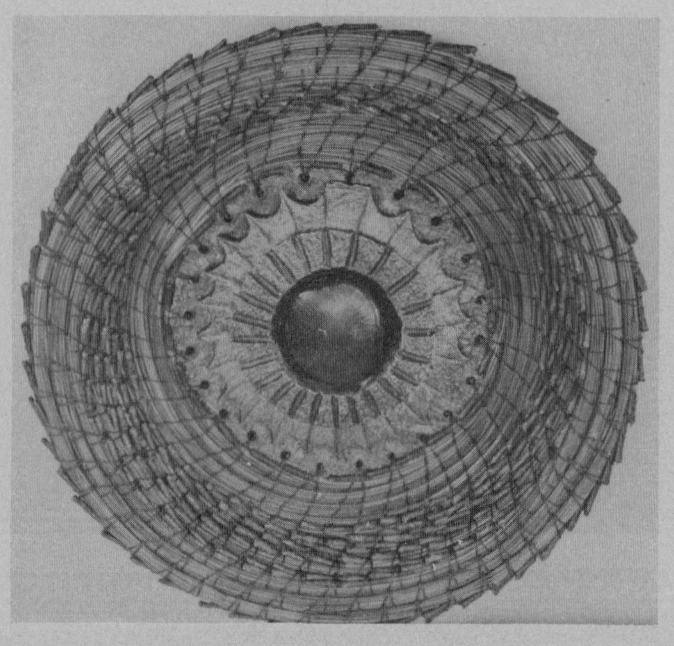

Tray shape - pine needles (dyed), waxed M. liner, pod, wax, paint; 11" wide x 2" high.

Stitches
5

~ STITCHES ~

Each stitch that you use creates its own pattern. It can be used by itself or combined with other stitches to enhance the baskets' appearance and to help give it stability.

Millie Kenner · 12" wide × 14" high. Montezuma
Pine needles, raffia ~ photo artist

You will always be working from the RIGHT to the LEFT and your needle will always be piercing the basket from the front or right side half way down in the bundle. Working this way enables you to have complete control over your needle placement. The stitches should be kept about 5/8 inches apart in straight work and 1/2 inch apart if working in a circle.

In the previous section we used the simple straight and split stitch to make our Basic Basket.

~STRAIGHT STITCH~

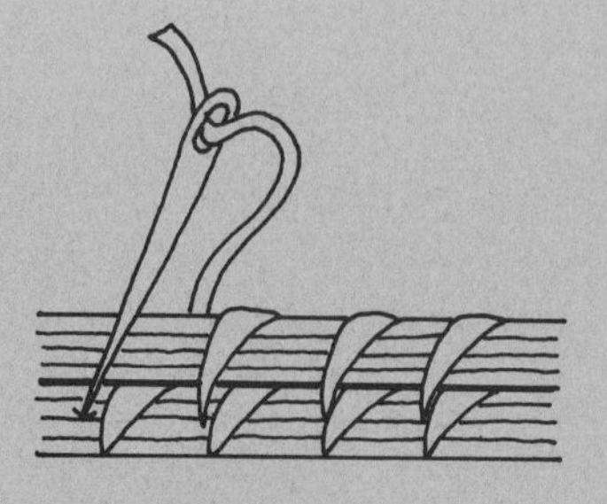

Also called: whip, plain and rope stitch. Insert the needle from the FRONT to the BACK to the LEFT of the stitch below and half way down in the bundle. Push the needle straight through the bundle

~SPLIT STITCH~

Insert the needle from the FRONT to the BACK through the middle of the stitch below. Also called the chain stitch.

~

Here are some other stitches you can use in future baskets:

~ OPEN WHEAT STITCH ~

First row:

Make a basic Split Stitch by inserting the needle through the middle of the stitch below and half way down into the bundle. Then take another stitch into the same hole. This will give you a slanted and a straight stitch. Going twice into the straight stitch adds firmness which is important on rims and in making handles.

Continue around for one row.

Second row:

Insert the needle half way down and into the middle of the "V" formed by the slanting and straight stitch. Take another stitch in the same hole.

~ STRAIGHT WHEAT STITCH ~

Instead of inserting your needle in between the "V" stitch (see "Open Wheat Stitch" on previous page), insert the needle half way down in the MIDDLE of the VERTICAL stitch. Take another stitch in the same hole. This will give you a straight up and down stitch. If you are using a fiber that does not split, insert your needle just to the right of the vertical stitch.

← split stitch

← straight wheat stitch

JM - 7" wide × 6" high; Jeffrey pine needles, raffia, gourd, gourd seeds, dye, wax.

~SPIRAL WHEAT STITCH~

Make a basic Split Stitch, but this time take two stitches in the center of the slanting stitch.

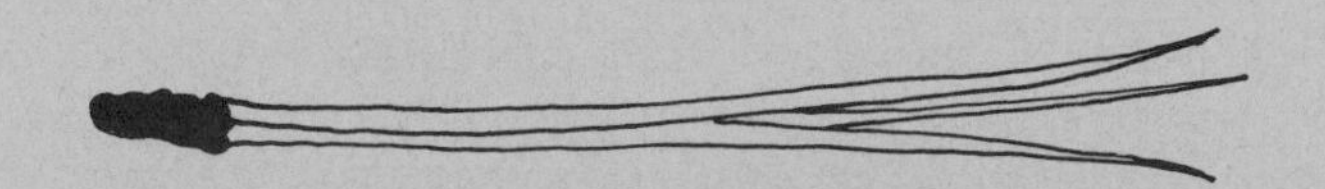

← teneriffe design

← wrapping

Marilyn Moore - 8" wide x 7½" high; pine needles, raffia; teneriffe design. (Photo Ted Ward).

~WING OR FERN STITCH~

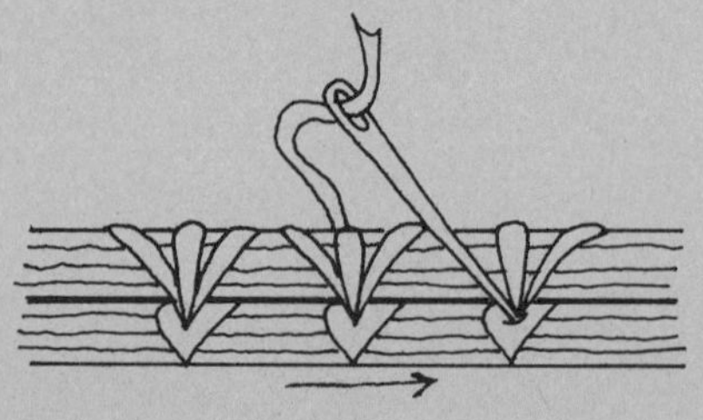

Do one complete row of the STRAIGHT Wheat Stitch. Then back stitch to the right taking a stitch into the base of your vertical stitch. Complete one row. This and the Popcorn stitch are the strongest stitches and are used when you need a lot of stability in your basket.

← wrapping

Millie Kenner - 14" wide x 6½" high; Montezuma pine needles, raffia, deer antler. (photo artist)

~POPCORN STITCH~

First row:

Make a Wheat Stitch (a double Split Stitch), but this time take several stitches into the same hole of the second or vertical stitch. Fan the stitches out. Complete one row.

Second row:

Back stitch to the right going into the same hole. This and the Wheat Stitch are very strong stitches.

~ INDIAN WRAP ~

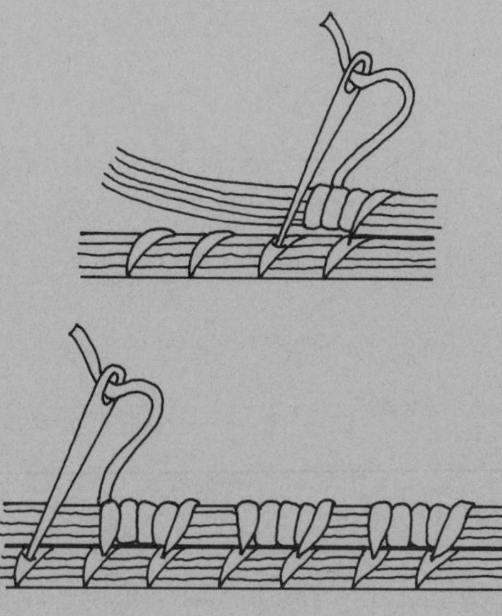

Make a Split or Straight Stitch. Then wrap your raffia around the bundle several times. Take another stitch and wrap again. Many different patterns can be made using this stitch.

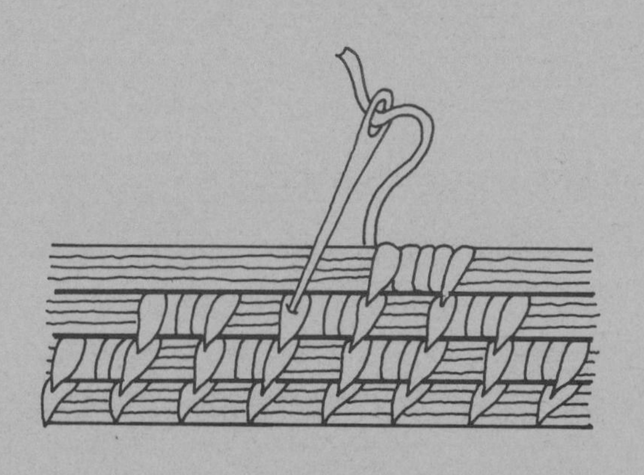

~LAZY STITCH~

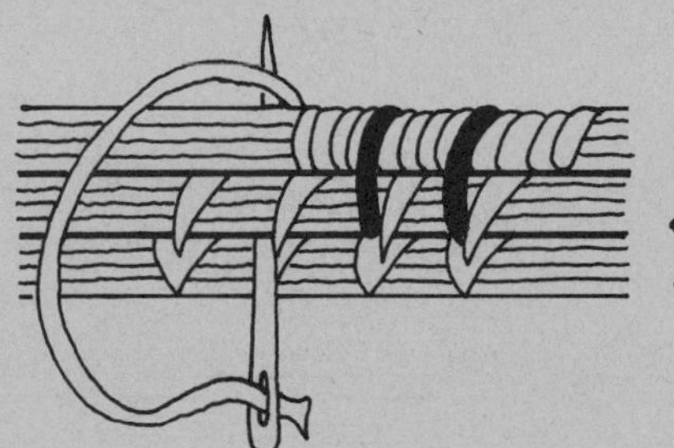

First row:

Make a long wrap with your raffia over the working foundation and the previous row. Your needle will go between the second and third rows. Wrap your raffia around the bundle several times and take another long stitch.

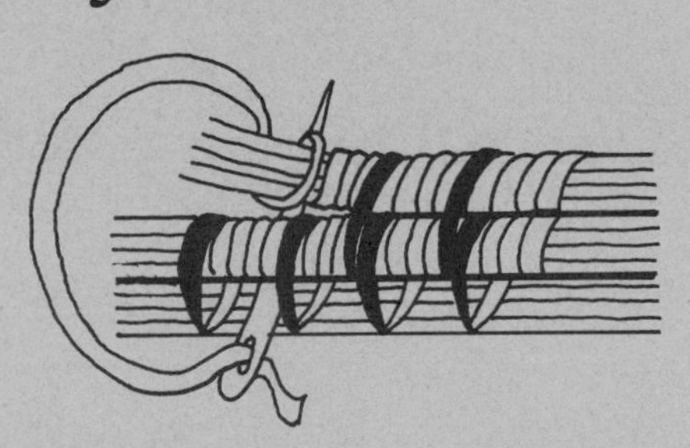

Second row:

Make your binding stitch to the LEFT of your previous stitch.

Or ~ only wrap after every other stitch. This will give you a checker board pattern (See pages 52, 61 & 70). →

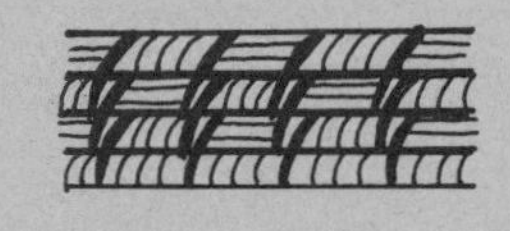

~ MARIPOSA (LACE) STITCH ~

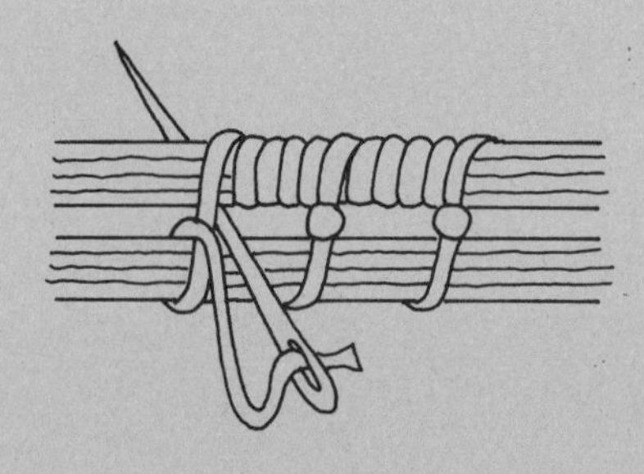

Make a Lazy Stitch, but this time wrap your raffia around itself between the rows.

Many different patterns can be created by varying the amount of wrappings and careful placement of the lace stitch.

~TUNOPONG STITCH~

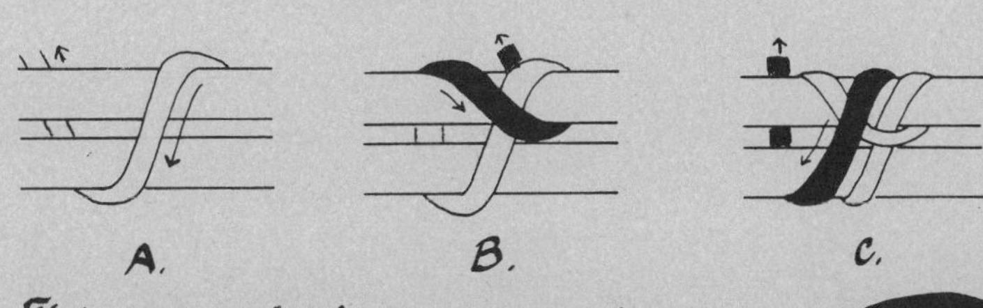

This stitch is an adaptation of a stitch used in the coiled baskets made by the Micronesians in the Caroline Islands. The Trukese call this stitch a "Tunopong" stitch.

First row: Make a Lazy Stitch (A). Bring the raffia around the back, over and around the top bundle and to the right of the Lazy Stitch between the rows (B). Make another long Lazy Stitch (C.) to the left of the first one. Bring the raffia around the back, over and around the top bundle, over the last two stitches and between the rows (D.) This completes one stitch.

Second row: (E) Complete only the first two steps (A and B), but make your Lazy Stitch to the left of the stitch below.

~ TIE OR KNOT STITCH ~

FIRST ROW: →

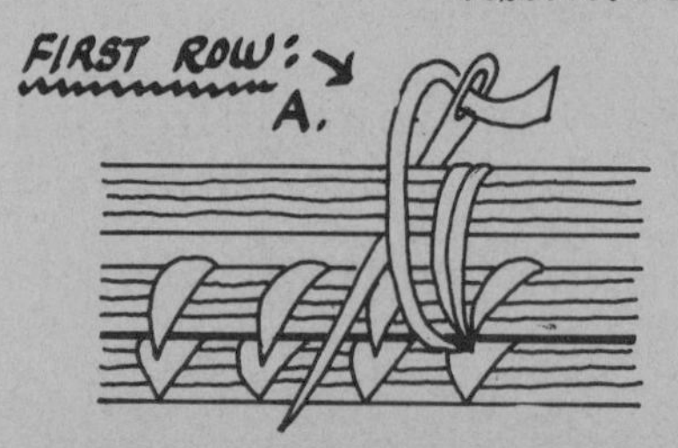

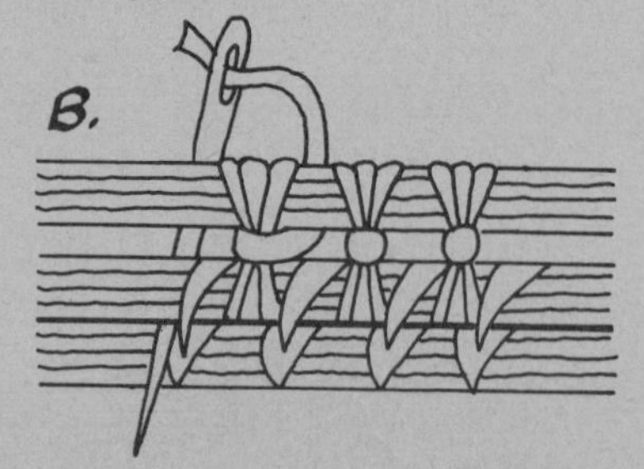

CHANGE NEEDLE DIRECTION:

(A & B) Wrap your raffia several times from front to back around and over the top two rows. Then wrap the raffia around itself between the rows. This completes one stitch. Insert the needle from the BACK between the second and third row. Wrap again...

SECOND ROW: →

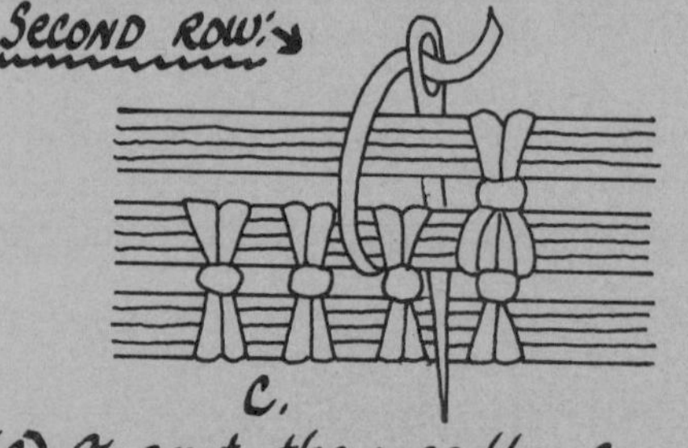

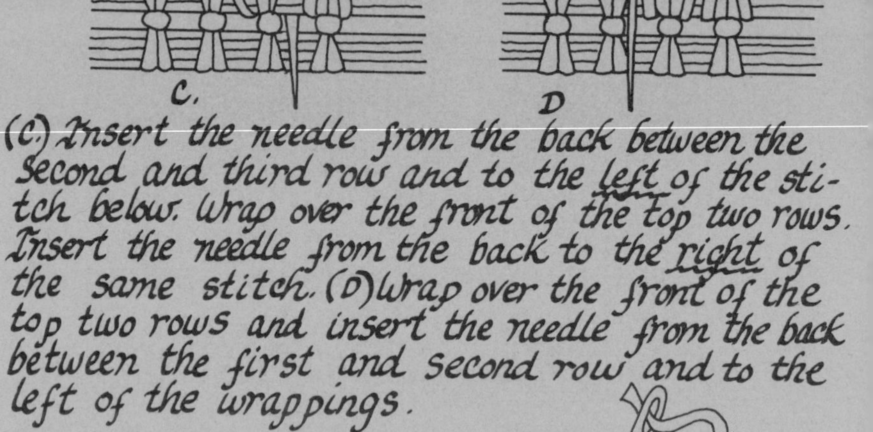

(C) Insert the needle from the back between the second and third row and to the left of the stitch below. Wrap over the front of the top two rows. Insert the needle from the back to the right of the same stitch. (D) Wrap over the front of the top two rows and insert the needle from the back between the first and second row and to the left of the wrappings.

(E) Wrap the raffia around itself between the rows. Go to the next stitch. →

~ WRAP STITCH ~

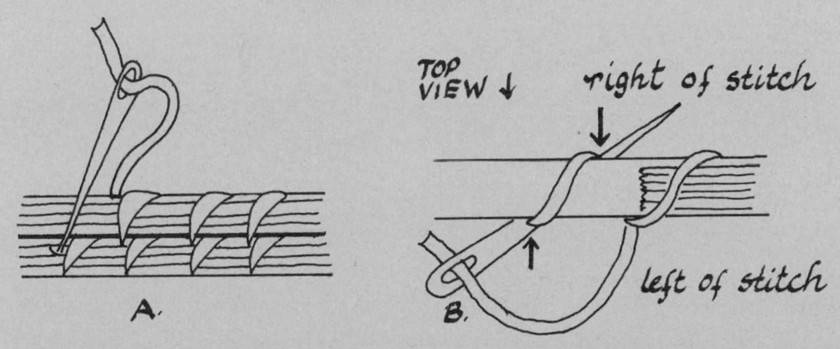

Make a simple Straight Stitch (A.), but angle your needle to the right through the bundle so it will come out to the right of the stitch on the back (inside) - B. This will give you a spiral pattern on the outside and the inside.

Millie Kenner - 10" wide x 7" high; Montezuma pine needles; waxed nylon.
(photo artist)

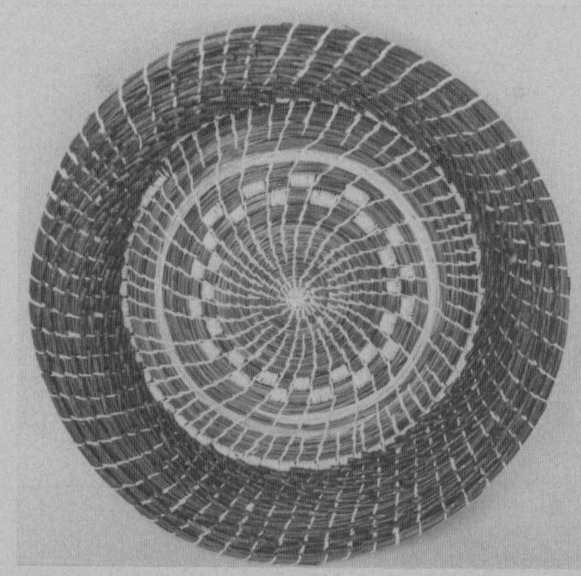

JM ~ 11" wide x 2½" high; dyed pine needles, waxed linen.

JM ~ 10½" wide x 6" high; dyed pine needles, waxed linen, wool, clay. Straight Wheat Stitch with the straight stitch placed to the right of the vertical stitch below.

6

~ENDING AND ADDING BINDING MATERIALS~

There are many ways to end and add binding materials. The main thing you need to be aware of is that you want to hide your knots or ends and you want to maintain the same angle with your stitches. You may use some of the following suggestions for ending and adding or you can make up your own way.

(1.) One step ending and adding:

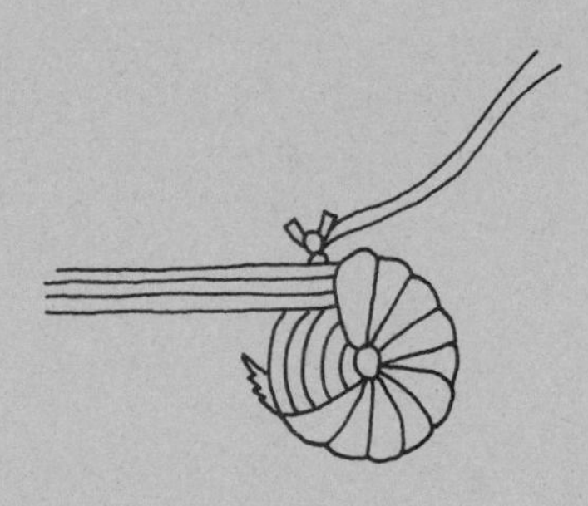

The "easiest" way to end and add a material is to tie a square knot with the old and new ends. Make sure that the knot sits squarely on top of the row so it will be covered by the next row.

② Scoop Stitch:

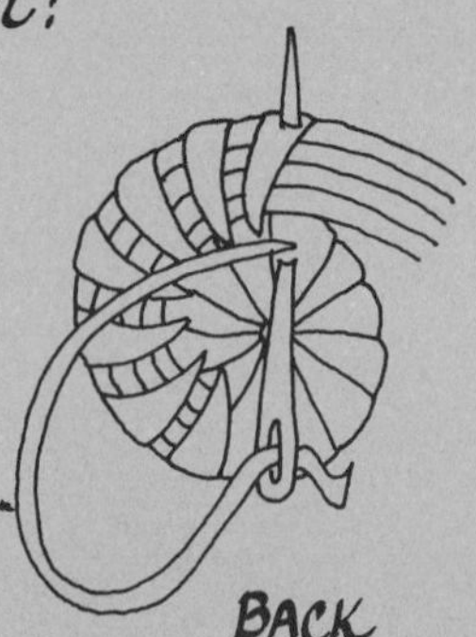

BACK

ENDING: Turn the basket around to the back. Make a Scoop Stitch under where the needle just came out and push the needle up through the top bundle and through the previous stitch.

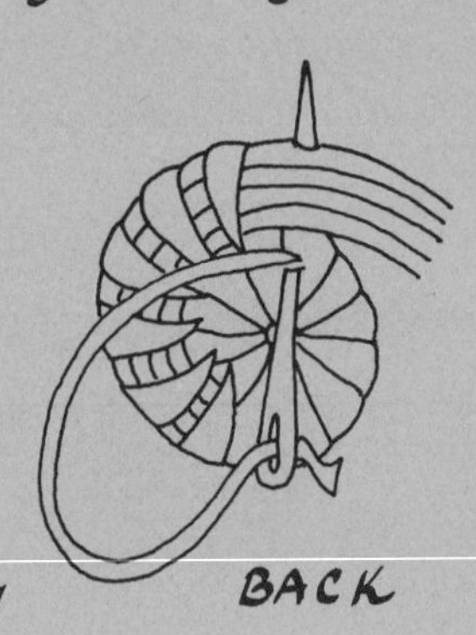

BACK

Or ~ just push the needle straight up into the bundle.

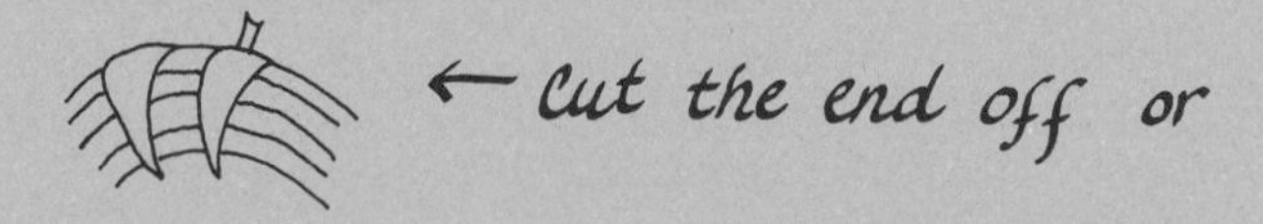

← Cut the end off or

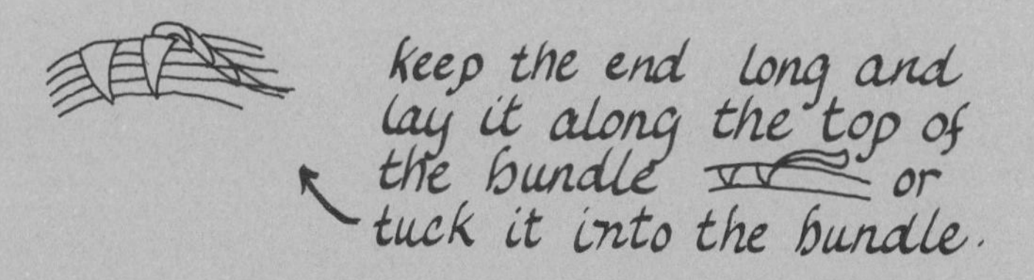

keep the end long and lay it along the top of the bundle or tuck it into the bundle.

ADDING:

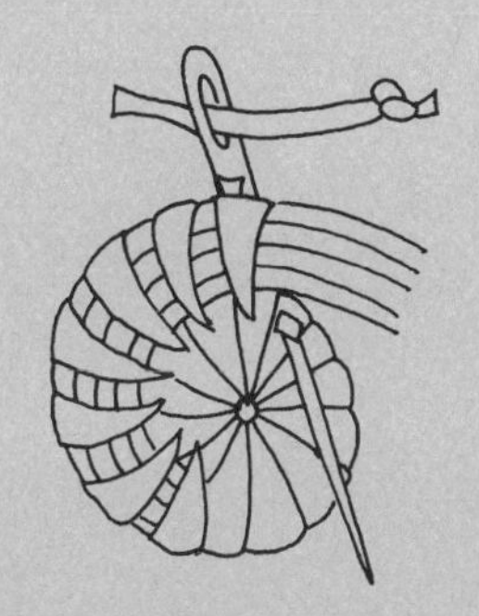

BACK

Make a small knot on the end of the binding material (raffia). Insert the needle in the middle of the last stitch on TOP of the bundle. Push it through the top bundle down into the next bundle and come out in the hole on the Back where you took your Scoop Stitch.

Or, insert your needle directly into the bundle →

BACK

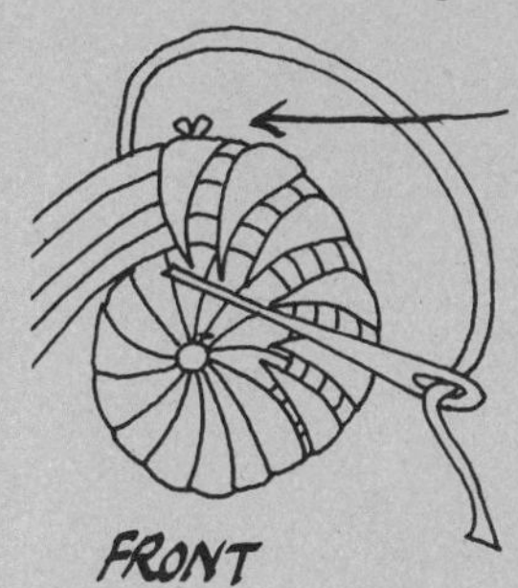

FRONT

Knot - If you use a knot, it will be covered by the next row. On the last, rim row (or, for all rows), pull the knot down into the bundle

No knot - leave the end long and lay it along the top of the bundle or twist it with the end of the old piece and push it into the bundle. →

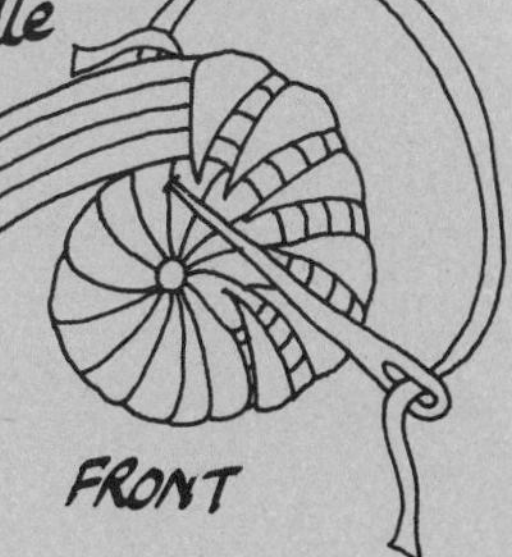

FRONT

③ ENDING: →

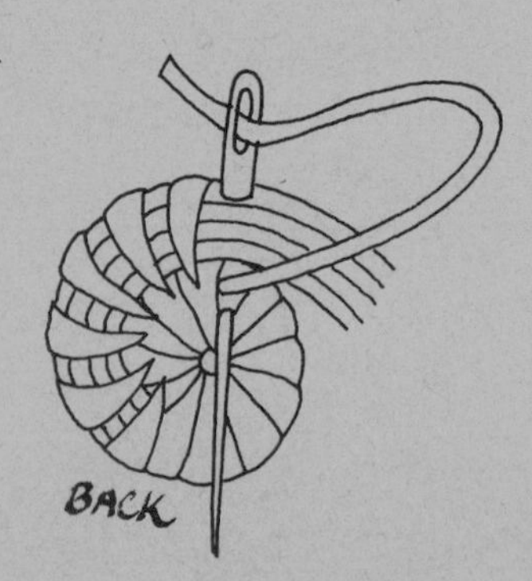

Insert the needle on the top of the bundle. Push it down through the top bundle, down into the next bundle and come out on the BACK below your previous stitch.

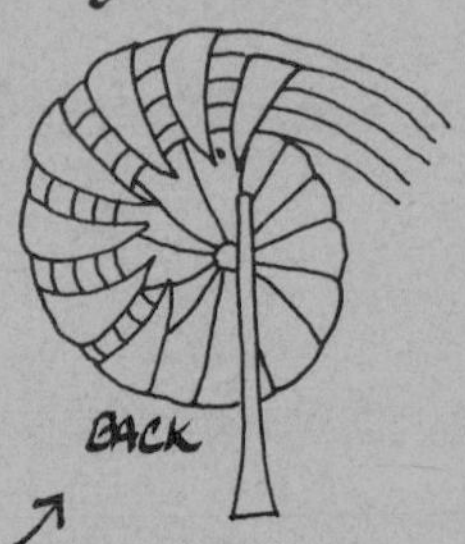

Trim the end after you have taken a few stitches.

ADDING: →

Insert the needle on the top of the bundle and through the half stitch you just made. Push the needle through the top bundle, down into the next bundle and come out on the BACK where you ended.

④ ENDING:

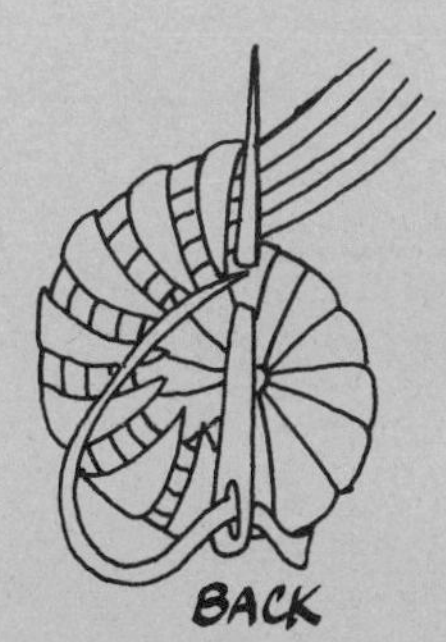

Make a small Scoop Stitch, but come up between the rows. Cut off the end or lay it along the top of the bundle.

ADDING:

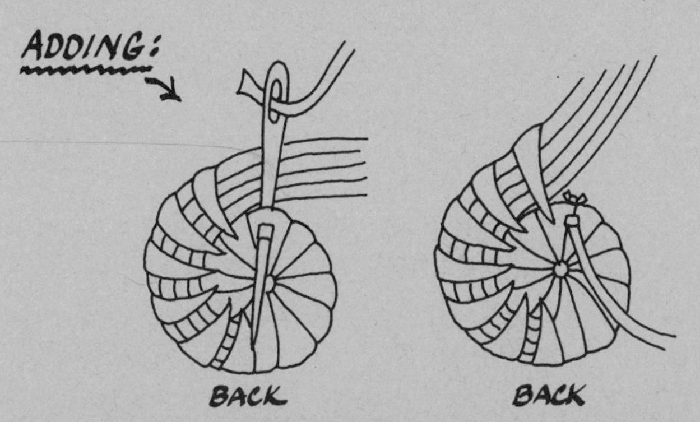

Insert the needle on top of the previous row where you ended your stitch and come out on the BACK where you took your Scoop Stitch.

⑤ ENDING:

Insert the needle on top of the previous row (between the rows) and push the needle down through several rows coming out on the BACK. Cut off the end.

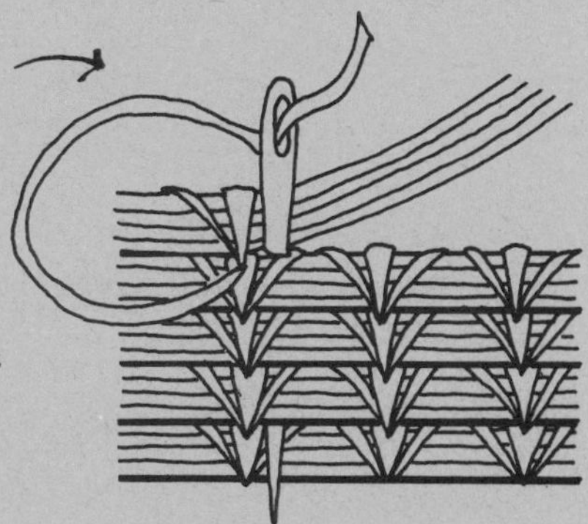

6 ADDING:

On the FRONT, insert the needle through the base of the stitch you have just taken. Pull the knot gently into the bundle.

7. ADDING RAFFIA ON THE DOUGHNUT OR OTHER WRAPPED AREAS:

I.

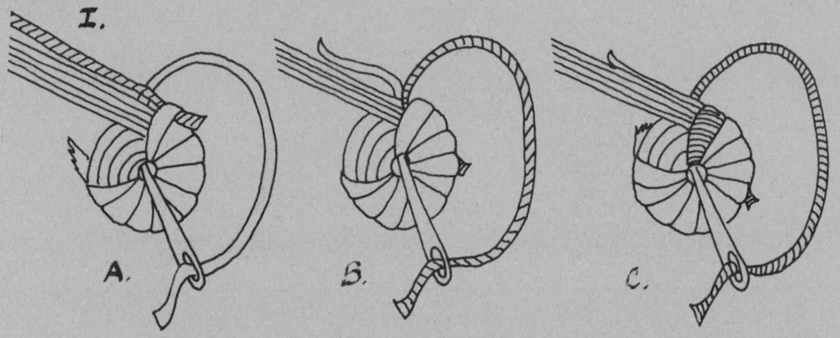

(A) - Lay a new piece of raffia on the top of the bundle and wrap over it several times with the old raffia. (B) Lay the old raffia end on the top of the bundle and wrap over it with the new raffia (C).

II.

ENDING: Push the needle up through the middle of the bundle and cut the end off.

ADDING: Push the needle up through the same hole in the middle of the bundle. Pull the end into the bundle or leave long and cut later. Wrap over the last stitch.

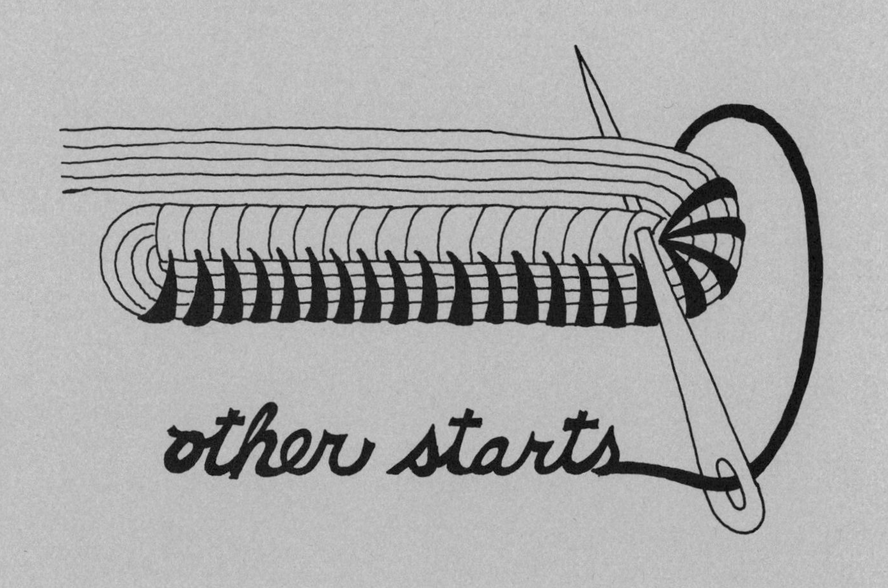

7

~OTHER STARTS~

There are many ways to start a coiled basket. In Chapter Four, directions were given for making the "Doughnut". Here are some other ways:

WRAPPED OVAL START:

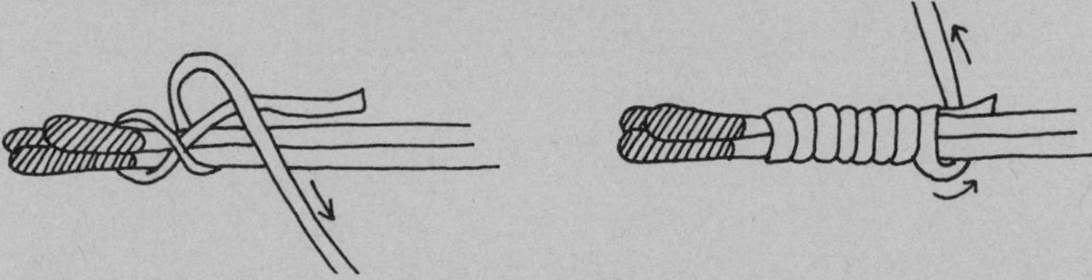

Take a pencil sized bundle of presoaked needles. With the sheath ends pointing to the left, wrap your raffia over and around the bundle from back to front and from left to right.

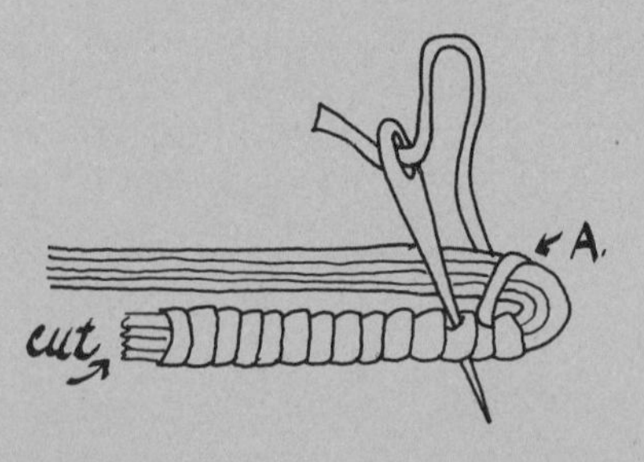

When you have wrapped 1 to 2 inches, bluntly cut off the sheath ends. (If you want a very long oval beginning, you will have to feed the bundle). Fold the ends up and over the top of the wrapped section and take a "Stop Stitch" to hold the turn in position. (A.) Continue taking stitches from the FRONT to the BACK into the top THIRD of the bundle. Evenly space your stitches.

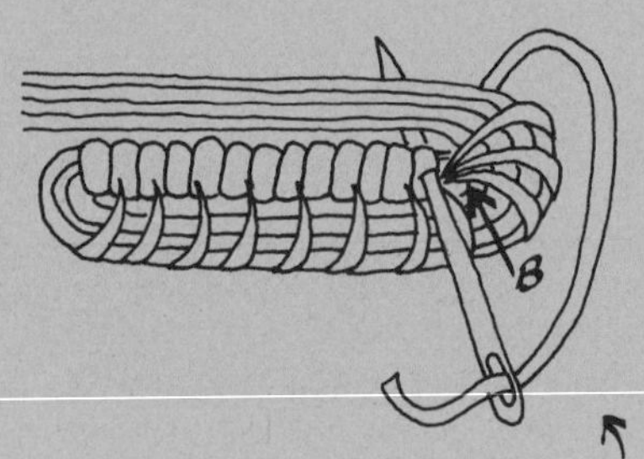

Turn the corner, covering up the cut off ends. Take several stitches in the same hole (B) and fan the edges out. Continue onto the other side. Feed your bundle when necessary. On the next row, continue with any stitch that you want.

KNOTTED START:

This is a very quick beginning and very easy to do.

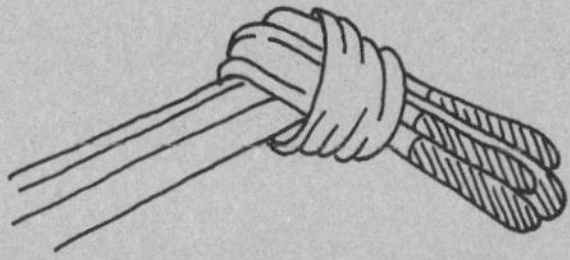

Take a pencil sized bundle of presoaked needles and tie the needles in an overhand knot near the sheath ends.

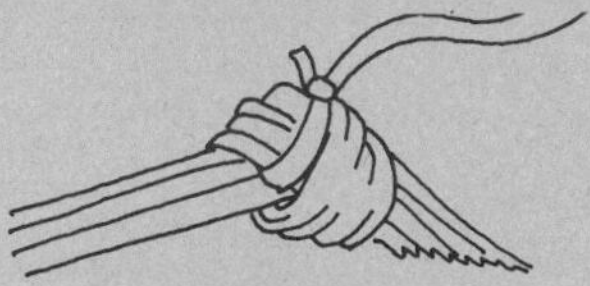

Tie a piece of raffia on the top of the knot and cut the sheaths off at an angle on the underside.

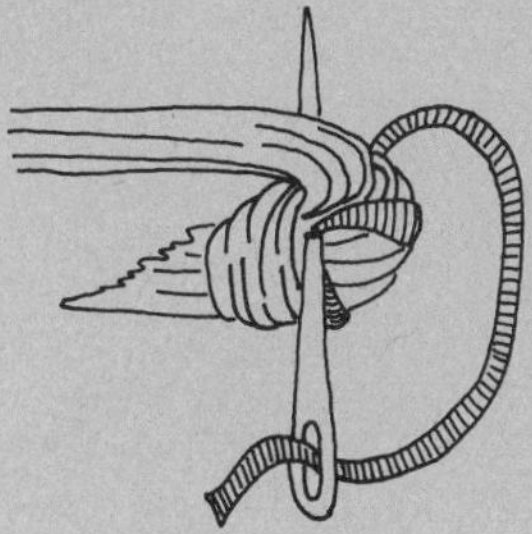

← Take stitches from the FRONT to the BACK through the middle of the knot. Go from the right to the left.

Catch in the cut ends as you go around. →

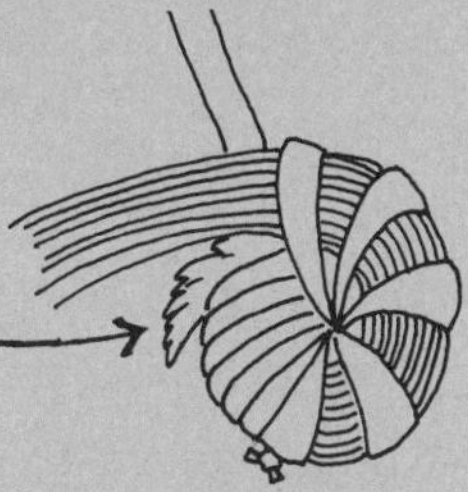

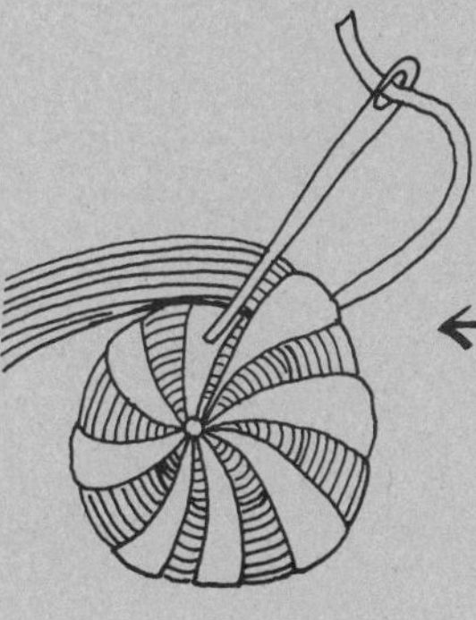

← Take a Stop Stitch after one row and proceed as with the Doughnut.

You can use other materials such as wood, bark and clay for the bottoms of your baskets.

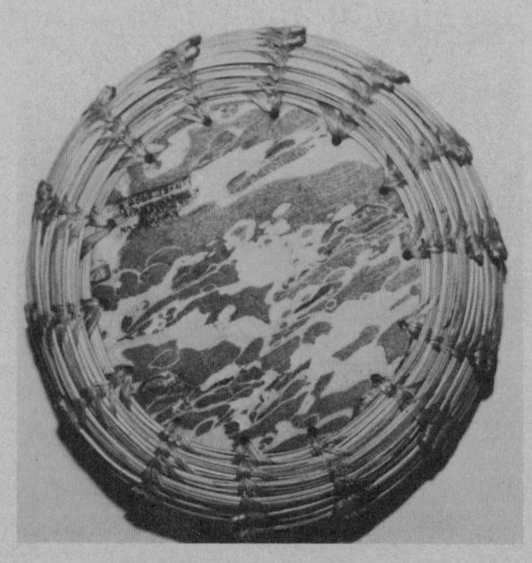

All you need to do is to add holes ¼th to ½ inch apart around the edges to hold the stitches.

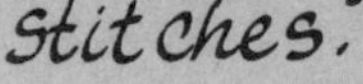

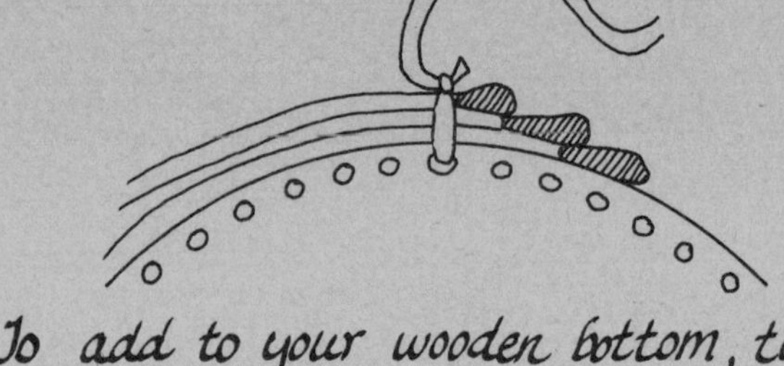

To add to your wooden bottom, take a pencil sized bundle of dry needles and lay the staggered sheath ends along the rim of the disk bottom. Double knot a piece of raffia around the bundle near the sheath ends. Keep the knot on the top. Take a second stitch in the same hole going from FRONT to BACK.

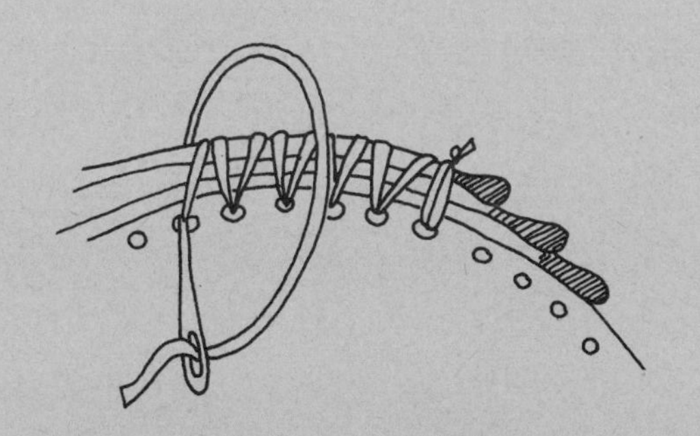

Go on to the next hole and take two stitches in that hole. This will give you a Wheat Stitch.

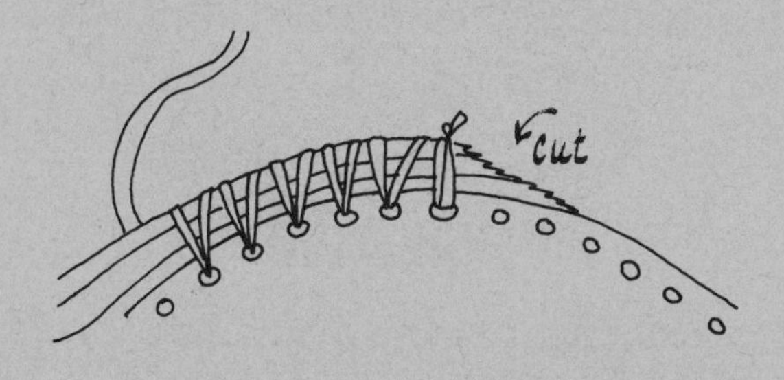

After five or six stitches, cut the sheath ends off at an angle. They will be covered by the next row. On the next row continue with any stitch you want.

TENERIFFE STARTS:

Please refer to the following section.

SIGNING YOUR BASKETS:

You may want to sign and date your basket. To do this, coat a small section, usually on the bottom, with clear shellac or clear nail polish. Let dry. With a fine pointed black inked pen, write your name and date. Let dry and coat again with shellac or nail polish.

8

~TENERIFFE~

JM-Sampler basket-tray; 9" wide x 1" high; pine needles, raffia; teneriffe.

The origins of the modern Teneriffe designs go back to the embroidery (drawn thread or cut work) of the Middle Ages. These designs were popular in Spain in the 16th and 17th centuries where the medallions were called "sol" (sun) or "rueda" (wheel designs).

Lacemakers still live on the island of Tenerife, the largest of the Canary Islands off the N.W. coast of Africa, and the craft is a cottage industry. (Modern spelling for the islands is "Tenerife," but the traditional spelling is "Teneriffe".

Lace with Teneriffe designs.

During the 16th century this lace technique was brought to South America. The technique soon spread to other cultural groups who began incorporating the designs into their basketry.

A good example of teneriffe work is shown in the cowrie embellished baskets of the Marshallese, Ponapaens and Trukese of Micronesia.

← In this Trukese tray, prepared coconut leaf is used as a binder and to weave the teneriffe design. The core is thatch palm wrapped with pandanus.

In the United States, many different materials are used to make the woven designs, but raffia is the traditionally used fiber. The designs are woven on spokes attached to wire shapes.

WIRE SHAPES:

You can buy metal or plastic rings to make your designs on. Or you can make your own shapes using 16 to 18 gauge galvanized steel or copper wire that has been bent to the desired shape and the ends soldered. Wire shapes can be made by wrapping the wire around different diameter bottles or dowels or by pounding headless nails into a board and wrapping the wire around the nails.

PREPARING THE RING:

To give the spokes (warp threads) a foundation to attach to, a double button hole stitch is done around the entire wire shape.

DOUBLE BUTTON HOLE STITCH:

(A.) Split the raffia to 1/4th or 1/8th inch in width. Fold the raffia in half and place the loop over the ring pointing to the RIGHT.

A.

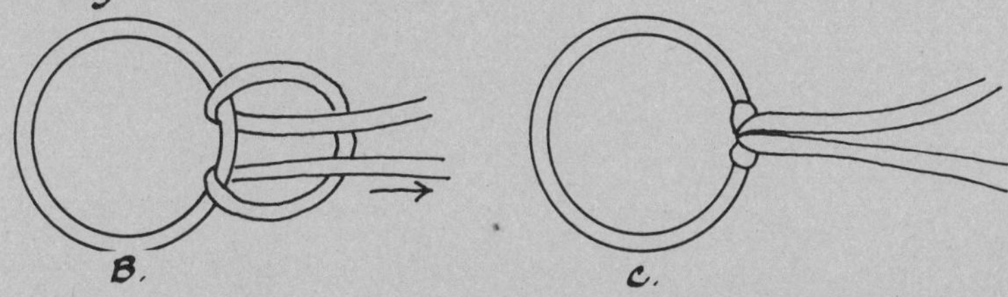

(B.) Put the ends down through the center of the ring and up through the middle of the loop. (C.) Pull the ends to the RIGHT. This forms a larks head knot.

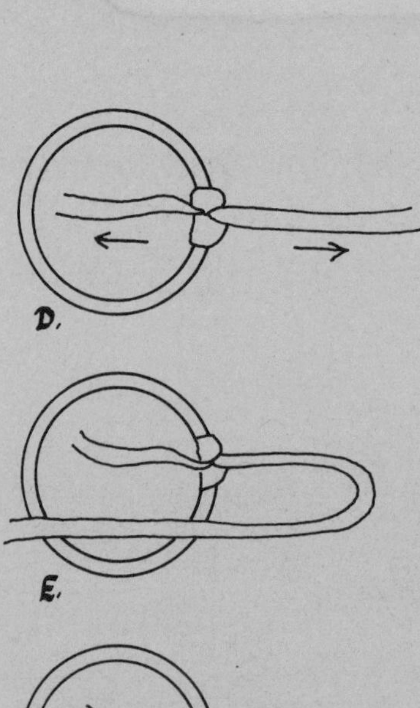

← (D.) Spread the two ends apart. The top strand goes to the RIGHT and the bottom strand goes to the LEFT.

← (E.) Take the RIGHT strand and form a loop over and to the RIGHT of the ring.

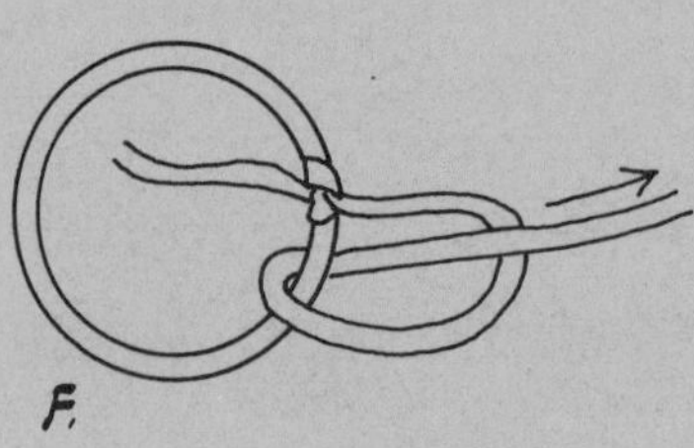

← (F.) Put the end down through the center of the ring and up through the middle of the loop and pull it to the RIGHT.

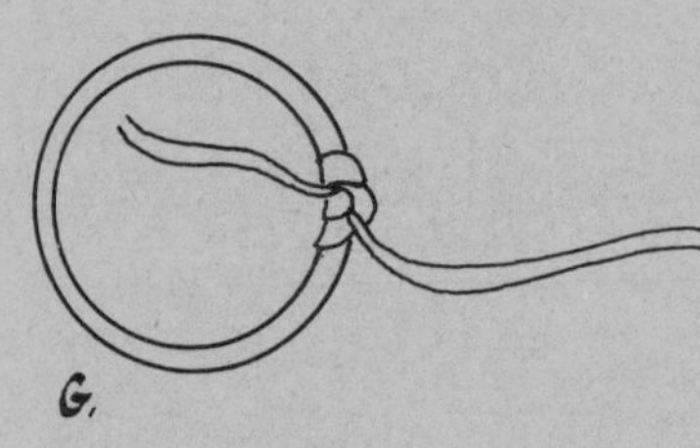

← (G.) Keep this knot on the outside of the ring.

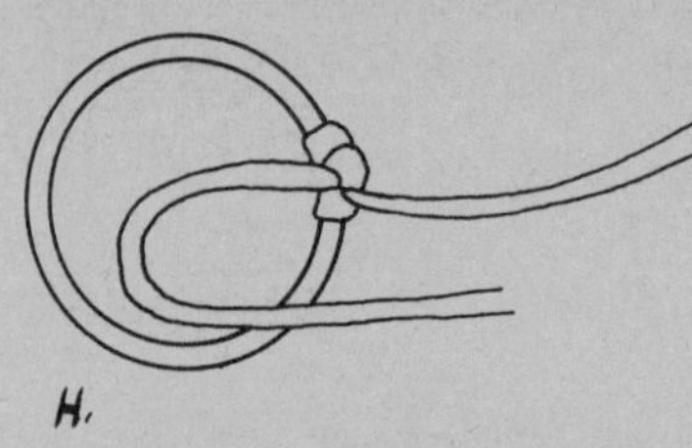

← (H.) Take the LEFT strand and form a loop over and to the left of the ring's edge.

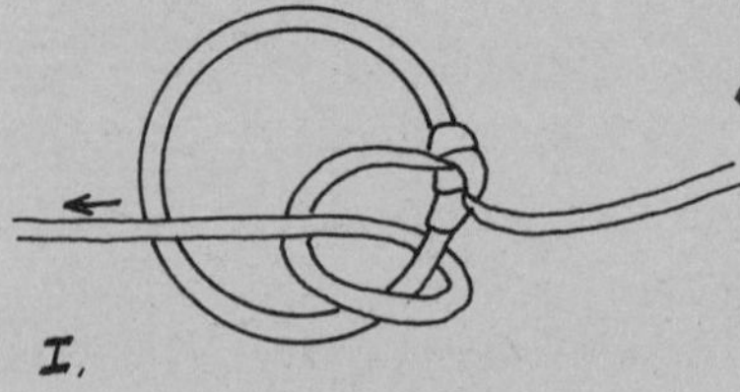

← (I.) Put the end around and under the ring edge and up through the middle of the loop and pull it to the LEFT.

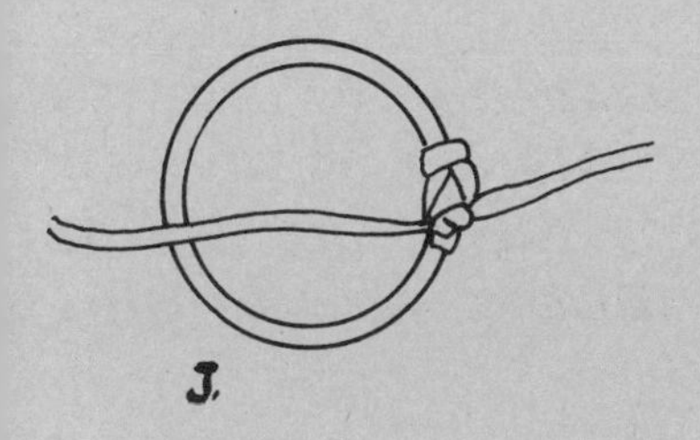

←(J.) keep this knot on the inside of the ring.

ADDING NEW RAFFIA TO THE RING:

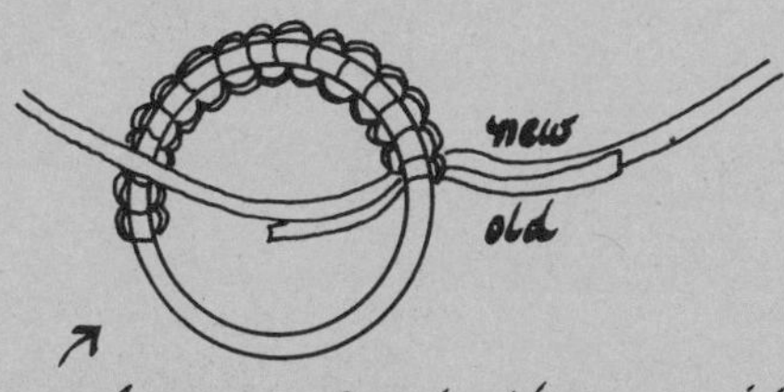

When you have about three inches of raffia left, you need to add a new length. Place the middle of a new piece of raffia under the ring and the last knot and lay the old ends with the new ends. Treat the old and new strands as one element and continue knotting for 3 or 4 knots. Cut off the old ends.

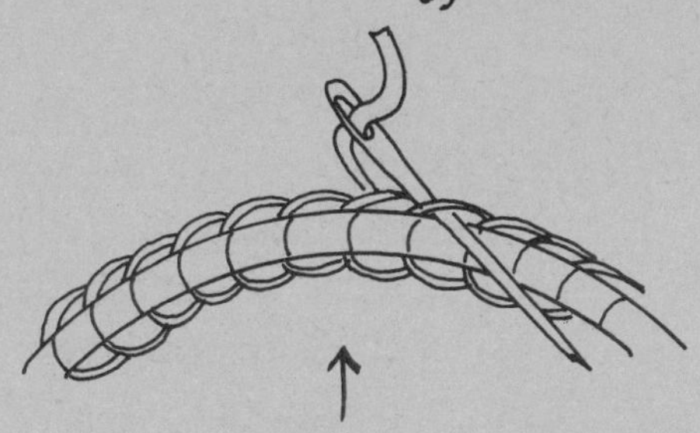

When the ring is covered, thread the right strand onto a needle and weave it into the outer edge for several stitches. Do the same for the left strand on the inside edge. If the strand is very long, do not cut it, but thin it down and use it for the spokes.

SPOKES:

The design is created from the amount of spokes that you use. I will use 20 spokes to illustrate, but any amount can be used. Thread a length of raffia 1/8 inch wide. The outer curled edge of the raffia is good. To secure the end, weave it in and out of the out side button hole loops for several stitches and for several more on the inside edge.

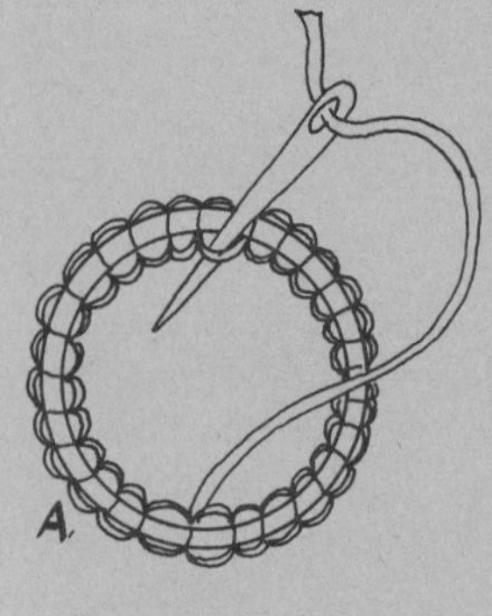

← (A.) Hold the ring with the raffia on the bottom. Bring the raffia to the front or right side of the work. Bisect the ring with the raffia and take a stitch on the opposite side from the FRONT to the BACK through one of the button hole loops.

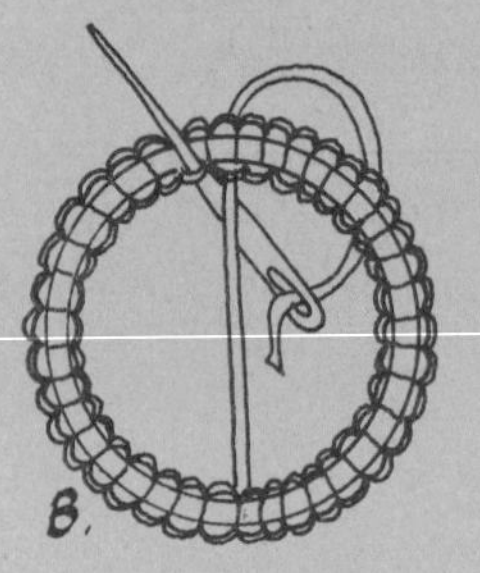

← (B.) On the back, take a small 1/8th inch "jog" to the LEFT and come up through another loop from the BACK to the FRONT

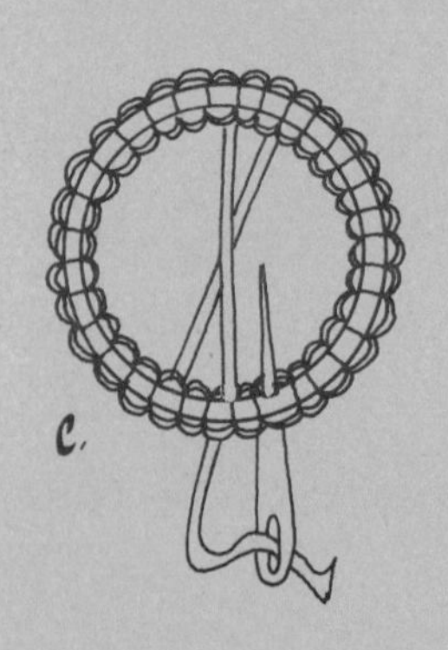

(C.) Bisect the circle again crossing over the first spoke. Insert the needle from the FRONT to the BACK in a button hole loop ← 1/8th inch to the RIGHT of the joining stitch. On the back, "jog" to the right 1/8th inch and take another stitch from the BACK to the FRONT. Continue bisecting the circle and crossing the spokes until you have 20 spokes or the circle is filled. REMEMBER to take the "jog" stitch on the back.

WEAVING:

You will begin to weave from the center out. If you have enough raffia left, lay it across the last spoke, bring it to the middle and wrap it around the spokes several times. OR: make a simple over-hand knot ....→ If you don't have enough raffia, finish it off by weaving it in and out of the out side button hole loops. Start a new piece in the middle by knotting the new end around the center spokes.

FOUR LEAF PATTERN:

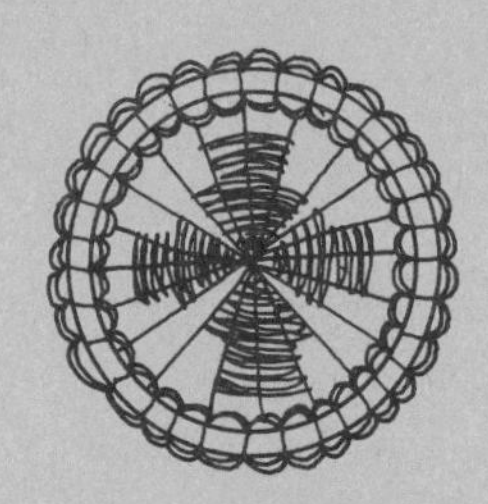

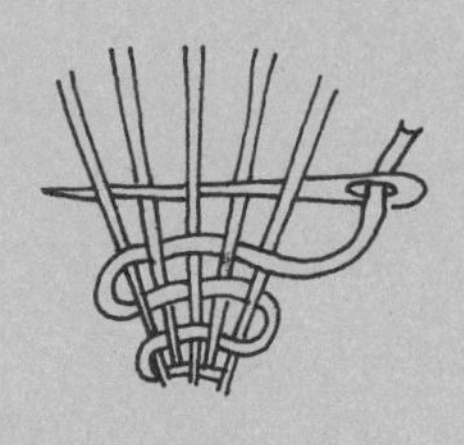

With 20 spokes on the ring, work from the center out across 5 spokes. Work from the left or right weaving over and under the spokes and back and forth for 1/4th inch or more. Drop one spoke on each side and continue to weave on the remaining three spokes.

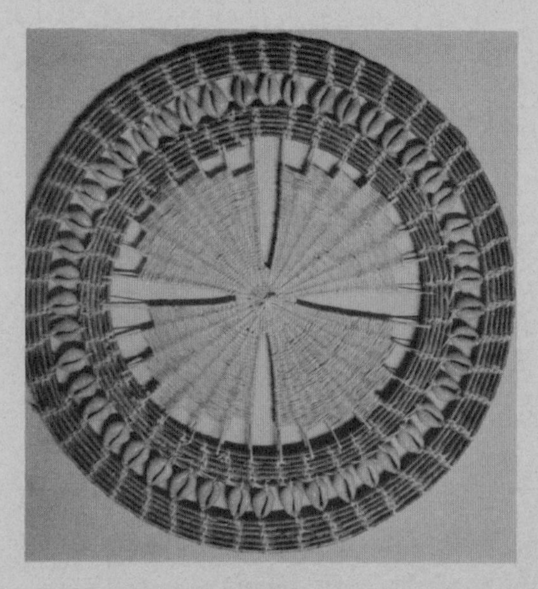

Trukese tray with Four Leaf pattern and more than 5 spokes per leaf.

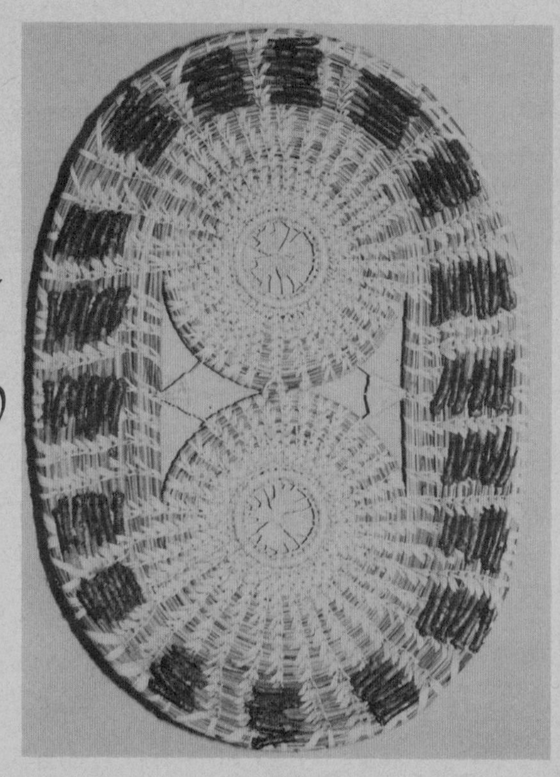

J.M.- Tray basket incorporating two simple Four Leaf, (5 spokes per leaf) teneriffe designs; Torrey pine needles, raffia.

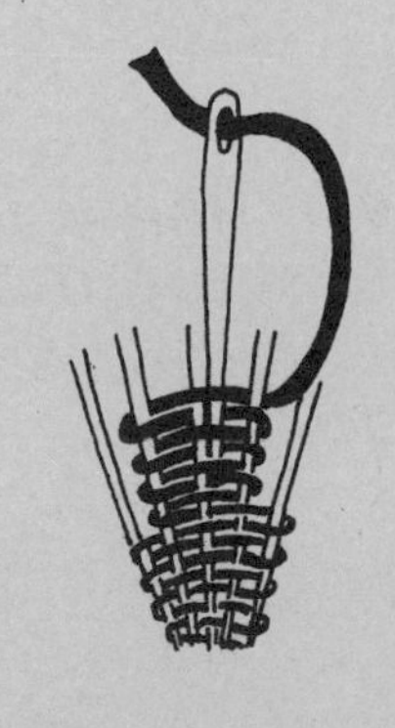

Return to the center by inserting the needle down the middle of the weaving and along one spoke. You will add new raffia the same way. Weave the next grouping of 5 spokes.

FOUR LEAF SWIRL PATTERN:

A.

B.

JM - Basket lid with 4 Leaf Swirl pattern and many spokes.

(A.) This time weave over and under the 5 spokes for several rows and then drop one spoke (or more - B.) on one side only. Weave several more rows and drop another spoke on the same side. Continue in this manner until the leaf is complete.

WOVEN CIRCLE:

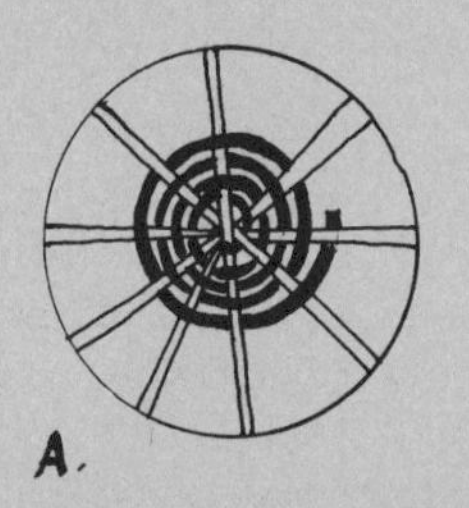

A.

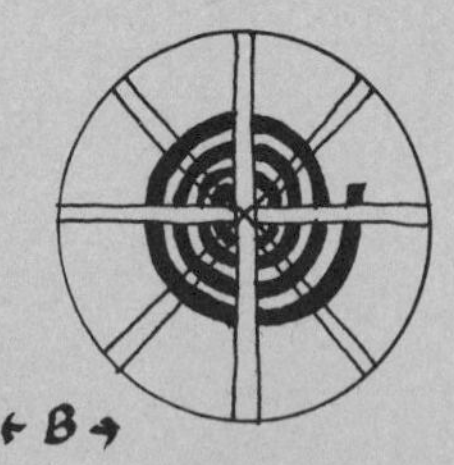

← B →

This is a simple design to do. It requires fewer spokes and you can use an uneven (A.) or an even number of spokes. You can weave just the center section or the whole ring.

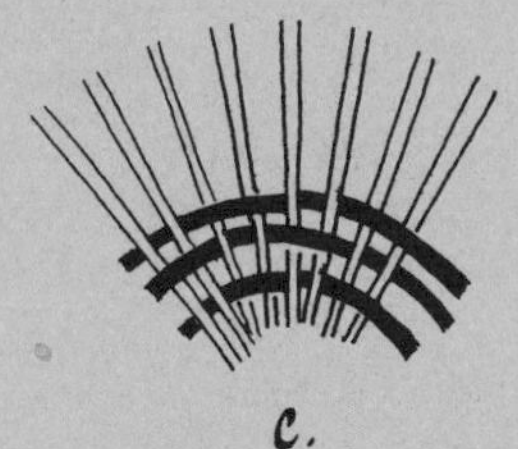

C.

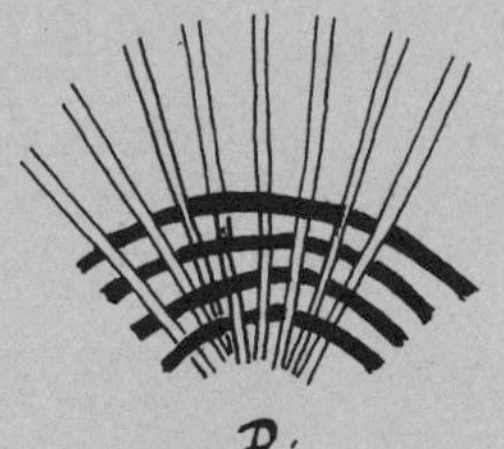

D.

You can do a simple pattern of weaving over and under one spoke (A & B) around and around the circle, or you can do twill patterns (C + D. - over 2 or 3 spokes in a staggered pattern).

ASYMMETRICAL DESIGNS: →

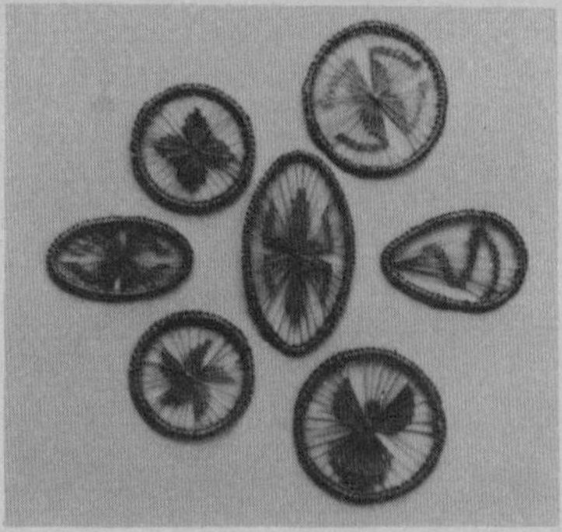

If you have trouble coming out with a certain number of spokes, try other designs. Be CREATIVE! Experiment.

Have all of your spokes radiating out from one point as in these Micronesian baskets: ↴

Use a lot of spokes and weave in the open areas around the main design.

JM

ADDING PINE NEEDLES TO THE RING:

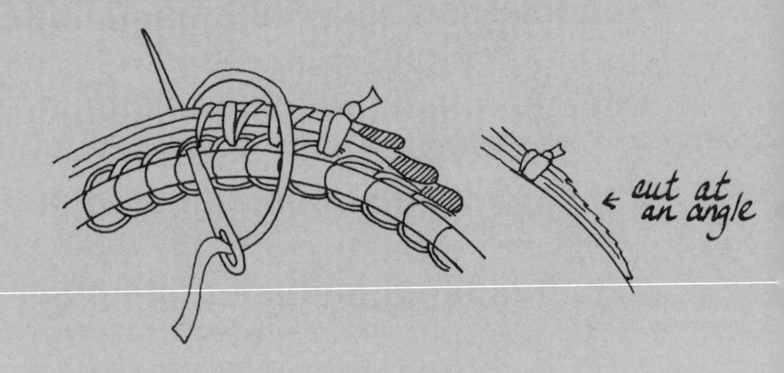

You will add the pine needles to the rim the same way you did for the wooden disk bottom (page 84), but this time you will take your stitches into the button hole loops.

Use your designs in all parts of your basket.

LIDS:

JM - 9" wide x 3" high; raffia; dyed pine needles; wax; paint.

BOTTOMS AND SIDES:

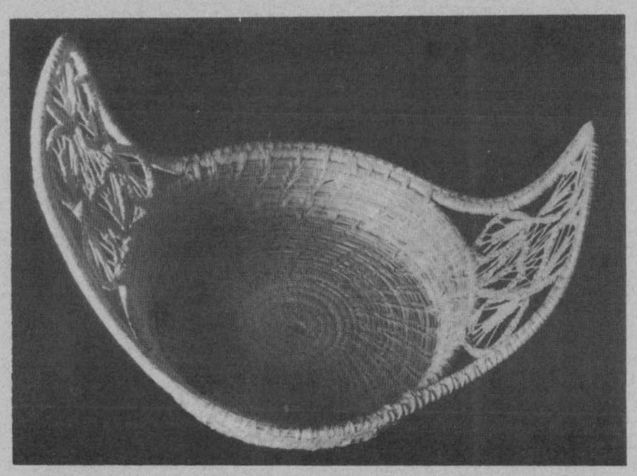

Jennifer Smith - pine needles, raffia.
photo - artist

Marilyn Moore - 11" wide x 2" high, pine needles, raffia (photo: Shereen La Plantz.)

lids

9

LIDS

If you want a lid for your basket, there are several types you can make:

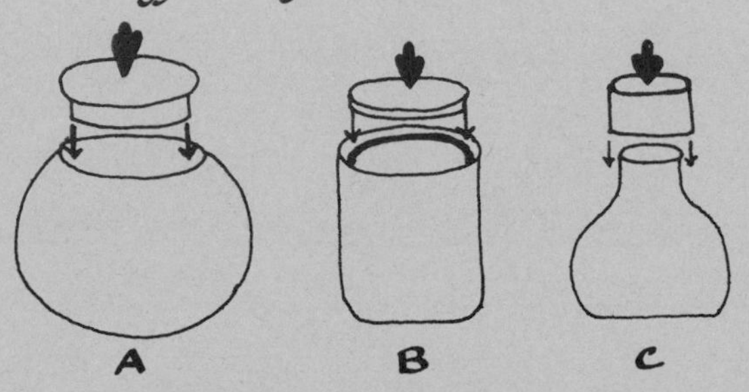

Ⓐ - The lid's lip sits down INSIDE the basket.

Ⓑ - The lid sits on a lip INSIDE of the basket.

Ⓒ - The sides of the lid fit OVER the basket.

LID A:

A fun top knot for this basket lid is one using the sheath ends.

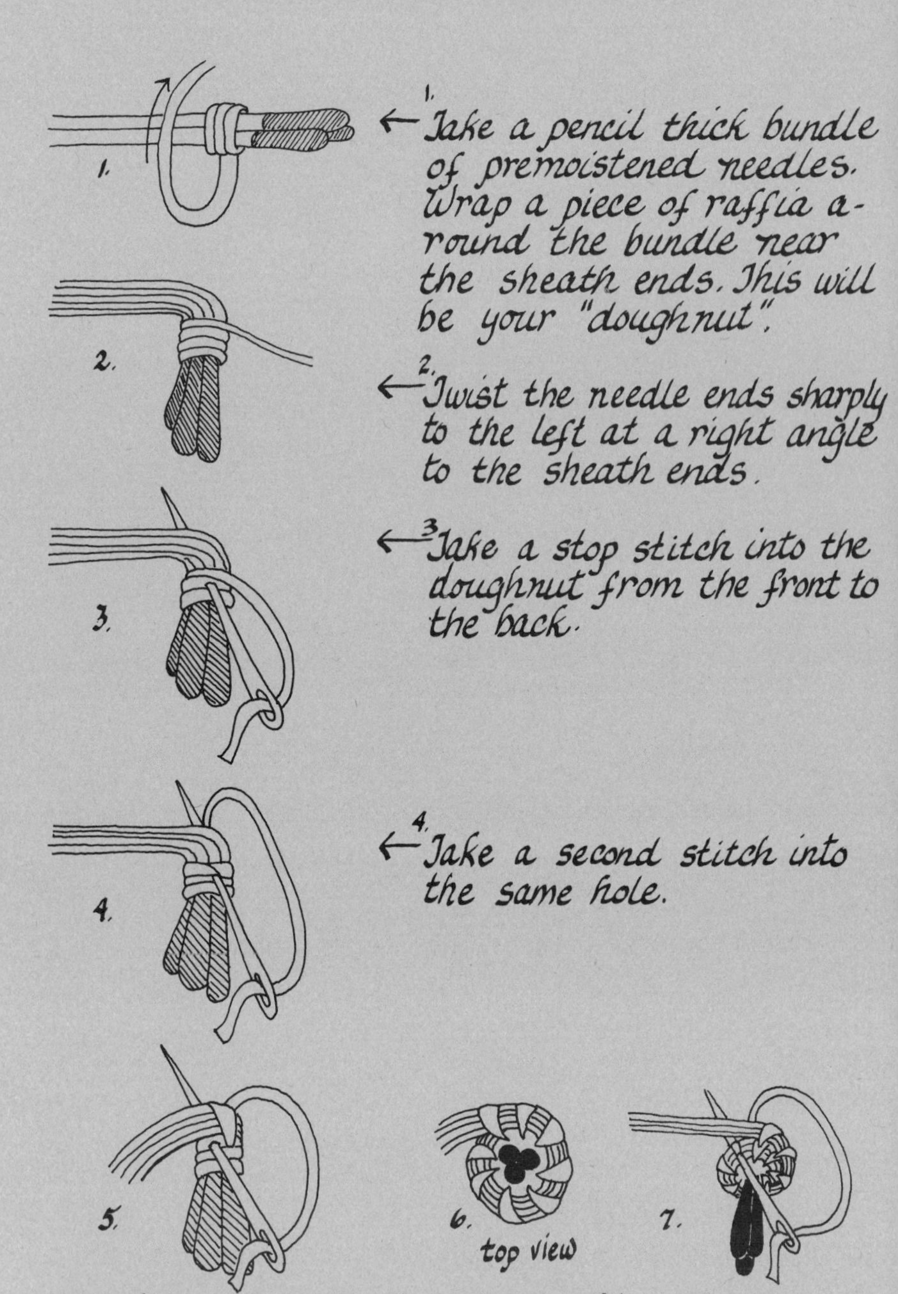

5-6: Keeping the needles at a right angle, continue taking more evenly spaced stitches around the doughnut. Feed the bundle when necessary. 7: On the second row use any stitch you want.

Continue enlarging the lid →
until it is almost the same
size as the mouth of the
basket and will drop into
the opening without touching
the sides.

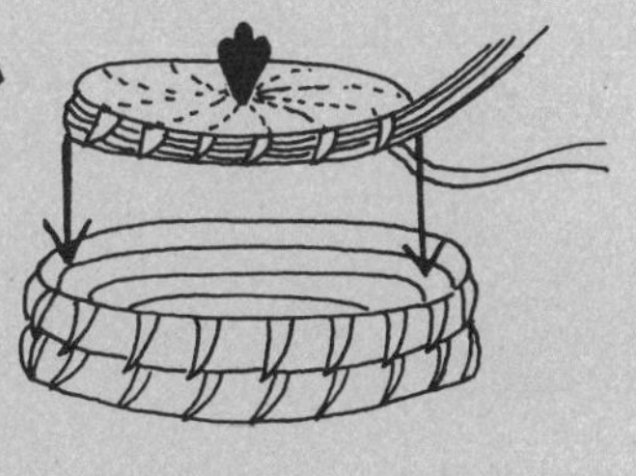

Turn the lid upside down.

THE LIP:

a

← wrong side

Split the bundle in half →

b

↖ right side

wrong side ↘

a

b

right side

← Place the top split section
(a) on TOP of the previous row
and on the wrong side of the
basket. Take a Stop Stitch. The
needle will be pointing UP.

Continue stitching around and around for two
or three rows depending on how
deep you
want the
lip to be.

lid
upside down

Keep feeding the bundle.
When you are two inches
from the ending point on
the last row, trim the needle ends at an angle
and finish the lip like you did the basket rim.

Turn the lid over so the right side is facing you again. Feed the half bundle that is left and continue to stitch as before. Do one or two rows and finish off.

Place the completed lid on the basket and tie the lid on with a piece of raffia. This will help the lid to shrink to fit. The split lip and tying techniques are used by the Pap-ago Indians in their coiled baskets.

LID B: For this lid, you must have stra-ight sides on your basket. Make and complete a lid that is just a tad smaller than the mouth of the basket and will drop into the basket. Attach your raffia to the basket with the raffia coming out two rows below the rim on the *inside* of the basket.

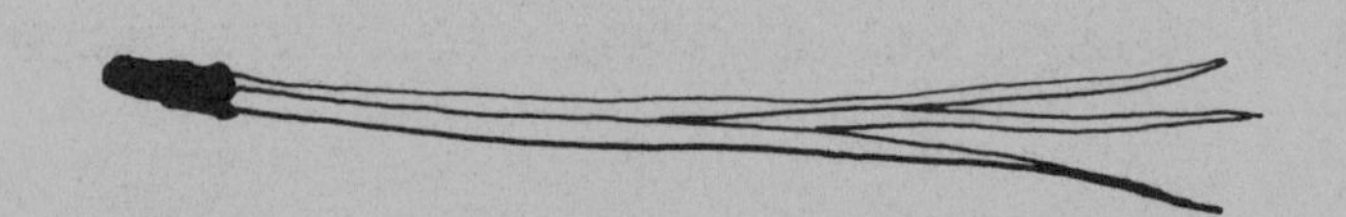

Take a pencil thick bundle of staggered needles with the ends cut off at an angle (a) lay them on the inside of the basket above the raffia. Insert the needle over the bundle from the back to the front. Come up on the

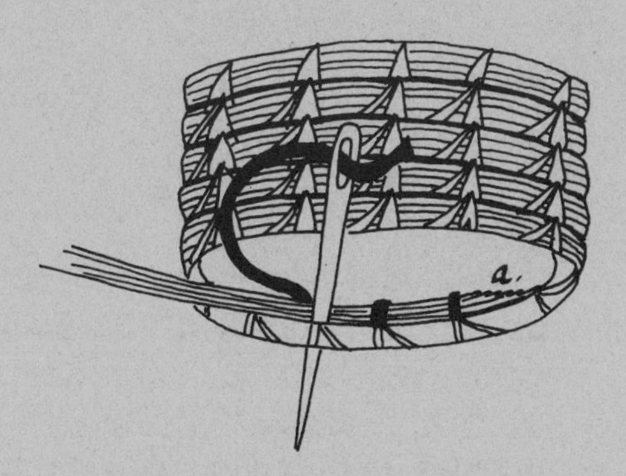

front at the top of a stitch. Then insert the needle at the bottom of the stitch and go from the front to the inside of the basket. Continue stitching and feeding the bundle until 2 inches from the joining. Trim the needle ends off at an angle and complete the row.

LID C:

JM -

If you have a basket with a neck, a simple top can be made by making a small basket with straight sides that will fit down over the neck. Make the disk top one row larger than the outside diameter of the neck and then make straight sides.

PINE CONE KNOB:

You may want to use a pine cone or some other object as a knob on your lid.

Wrap a piece of raffia →
around the base of a pine
cone forming a doughnut.

Insert the needle under →
the raffia once.

Repeat the first stitch, →
but bring the needle up
through the loop to make
a knot.

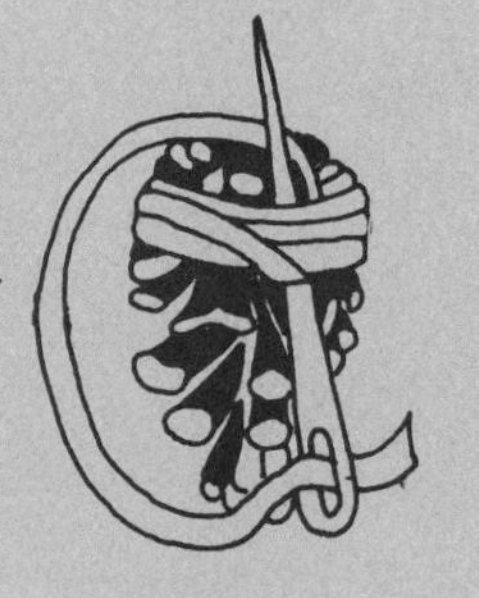

Lay a pencil thickness of
premoistened staggered needles
on the doughnut and below the
raffia. Wrap the raffia around the bundle
and take a stitch from the front to the back
through the doughnut. Take another stitch in
the same hole (wheat stitch.) After taking

4 or 5 stitches, cut the sheath ends off at an angle. Continue stitching around the doughnut for one row catching in the tapered ends. Use any stitch you want for the following rows.

Remember ~ you can use a teneriffe design on the lid. Be creative.

JM - 3" wide x 3½" high, pine needles, waxed linen, clay. "Ram Basket" with secret compartment inside the ram.

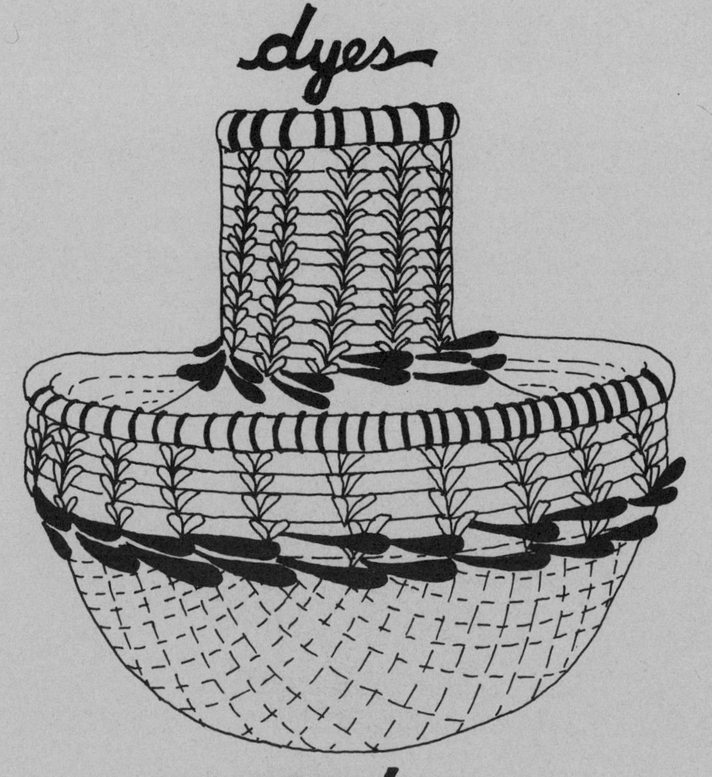

dyes and embellishing

10

~DYES AND EMBELLISHING~

JM - Janus Basket - 11½" x 9" x 7" high, dyed pine needles, waxed linen, clay, wax, paint.

This is the exciting section. You have learned the techniques of making the Basic Basket, so now you can explore the endless challenges of incorporating color and embellishments in your baskets.

REMEMBER: This is YOUR basket so you can do anything you want with it.

DYEING:

You can preserve some of the green color in your needles without dyeing them. Collect the needles green and dry them for two to three weeks away from the sun.

If you have dry needles and want more color you will have to dye them with either synthetic or natural dyes. You really need to experiment with several different dyes to get the effect that you want because different needles accept the dyes differently.

IMPORTANT: Before you dye the needles, wash, rinse and soak them. After they have been dyed, dry them thoroughly in the shade and then resoak them when necessary. The needles absorb too much water during the dyeing process and if they are used at this time, they will shrink causing the stitching to become very loose.

JM - Kitty Basket - 5" wide x 5½" high, dyed pine needles (some sheaths removed), waxed linen, clay, paint, wax.

Ways to dye:

1. Complete submersion - Dye the whole cluster with the sheath end on. Leave the sheath on or remove it to show the lighter, undyed tip (See "Kitty Basket" above). Or, remove the sheath before dyeing so it will be dyed also.

2. Graduated dyeing - Dip small bundles of needles into different levels of varied dye baths. Or, submerge the whole bundle for 10 minutes and then lift only 1/3 to 1/2 out of the dye for another 10 to 15 minutes. Experiment...

3. Tip dyeing - If you only want to dye the tips, carefully tie a bundle of needles with the sheaths all at one end. Bring a small amount of dye to a simmer, turn the heat off and stick the sheaths in until you have the desired color.

DYES:

SYNTHETIC DYES: These dyes work beautifully on pine needles and are very easy to use. Make sure to wear rubber gloves, do not breath the dye powder or use your cooking pots, cover the counter and surrounding floor and scrub up after you are finished.

Dye colors can vary depending on the amount of dye and water you use, the pine needles you use and how long they are left in the dye bath. I usually throw in a hank of raffia with each dye bath.

Here are some dye suggestions:

1. RIT ("Box Berries") This is an easy dye to use and produces strong colors. It is available in most markets in liquid or powder form and a wide range of colors. (You can also mix the dyes to get more colors.)

   COLOR: needles - sheaths and needles dye quickly and evenly a good, strong color; raffia - strong color with one side a little lighter.

   METHOD: Follow package directions. For darker colors I use the range top method and bring my dye bath to a simmer. After dyeing and rinsing thoroughly, I "set" the dyed needles in a vinegar bath for one half hour (1 cup vinegar to 1 to 2 gallons of water) and dry them thoroughly in the shade.

JM - "Midnight" - 11" wide x 11" high, dyed pine needles (some natural); clay bottom, waxed linen, wax.

2. CUSHING (available at weaving and craft stores). This dye will give you a completely different effect than RIT and you will wonder if you have actually dyed the needles... you have...

COLOR: needles - dyes the sheaths beautifully but only gives a subtle color to the needles; raffia - dyes dark on one side and light on the other.

METHOD: Follow package directions. I use the directions for "darker shades" and add ½ cup salt after 15 minutes of dyeing and then simmer for 30 minutes longer.

3. DEKA (sold in art and craft stores)

COLOR: needles - sheaths dye well and the needles grab the color better than CUSHINGS; raffia - uneven dying on both sides.

METHOD: Follow package directions. Simmer water and use more salt and less water; dye needs to be more concentrated for a darker color.

4. FIBREC - color effect similar to CUSHINGS.

COLOR: needles - sheaths absorb color well but only gives a subtle color to the needles; raffia - even dyeing on both sides; one side slightly darker.

METHOD: Follow package directions. The salt and fixer method barely works. Follow the directions for dyeing wool. Use hot water and vinegar instead of the fixer.

5. BASKETRY DYE - primarily for use on reed; color effect similar to CUSHINGS.

COLOR: needles - sheaths absorb color well but only gives a subtle color to the needles; raffia - dyes dark on one side and light on the other.

METHOD: Follow package directions.

6. DYLON (from England), color effect similar to CUSHINGS.

COLOR: needles - sheaths absorb color well but only gives a subtle color to the needles; raffia - dyes dark on one side and light on the other.

METHOD: Follow package directions; needs a DYLON Cold Fix package or one tablespoon household soda.

NATURAL DYES: There are endless recipes for natural dyes, but most use chemical mordants (alum, tin, chrome, etc.). Please refer to natural dye books for more information.

If you don't want to dye your needles, you can always stain or paint the ends ~ or, the whole basket if you want.

EMBELLISHING:

Let your imagination go. Combine dyed and undyed needles, embroidery, applique, beads, wood, clay, shells and found objects. Make your basket simple or complicated, traditional or sculptural, but, make it your own ~ the way You want it to be for You!

Here are some examples:

JM-"Dark Secret" series, 6½" wide x 8" high, dyed pine needles, waxed linen, clay, wax, paint.

Refined:

Marcie Stone - 7" wide × 8" high, pine needles, waxed linen, coconut shell, brass, horn. Beads were added during the weaving process. The needle goes from the back to the front.
photo - Kathy Wolfe.

Rustic:

JM - "Tarahumara Tribute" - 9" wide × 6" high, 5 kinds of pine needles, porcupine quills, dyed cotton string, clay, rush, bottle caps from Mexico.

Carol Booth - 11" wide x 9½" high, pine needles (dyed), waxed linen, clay; some sheaths removed.
photo artist

JM - "Fortune" - 9" wide x 8" high, clay, pine needles (sheaths are painted), waxed linen, dyed cotton string, dye, wax.

JM - 7" wide x 6" high, pine needles, raffia, gourd, gourd seeds, wax, dye, paint.

JM - "Bud" - 7" wide x 8½" high, dyed raffia and pine needles, clay, wax, paint.

JM - "Evolve 1A" - 14" wide × 5½" high, dyed pine needles, waxed linen, clay, wood, wax, paint.

~ SCULPTURAL ~

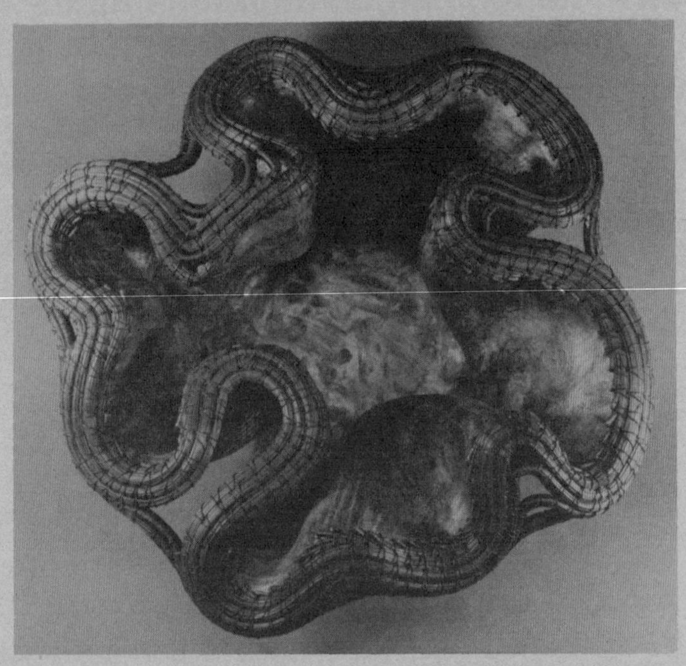

JM - "Evolve 4c" - 16" wide × 9" high, dyed pine needles, waxed linen, wax, paint.

Go large →

Philippine pine needle basket, 19" wide x 19" high.

Go small →

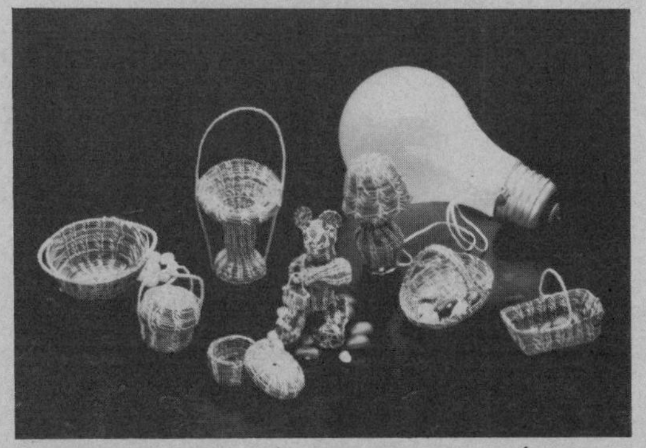

Nancy Oh-Bear is 3/4" wide x 2" high, pine needles, raffia. photo artist.

Rita Ploetz - turtle: 2" wide x 5/8" high; basket & lid - 5/8" wide x 5/8" high, pine needles, raffia.

~OTHER USES~

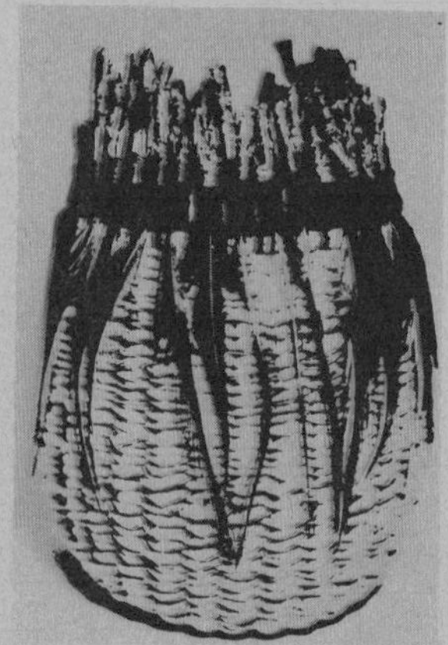

Betz Salmont - twined basket - 3½" wide x 5" high, pine needles, raffia, embroidery floss, feathers. photo - artist.

Wreath - Philippines - pine needles, 13" diameter
frame (U.S. ca 1920) 5" wide x 6½" long, pine needles.

trees

11

Pine Family
(Pinus pinaceae)

sheath

needles (leaves)

cluster

Pine trees are evergreen, monoecious conifers that are extensively cultivated. There are over 90 species of pines native to the Northern Hemisphere and many of their needles can be used in pine needle baskets.

The pine needles are the leaves of the tree and there are two kinds. The juvenile leaves are deciduous, solitary and scale like. From their axils grow the adult needles in clusters of 2 to 5 (one species of one needle) that are attached to the tree by a sheath and remain on the tree from 2 to 6 or 8 years.

The fruit of the tree is the cone. They are woody with bracts and some have prickles and spurs.

On the following pages are pictures and descriptions to help you identify some of the trees with long needles usable in pine needle basketry. Shorter needles may be used, but the longer the needle, the easier it is. Also, remember you can use several different needles in one basket. It depends on the effect that you want. Each tree species has its own unique needle cluster. Some are long and skinny with a delicate sheath and color (Canary Island Pine), while others are sturdy and have a large sheath (Torrey Pine).

Sometimes identification is difficult due to hybridization in the lower mixed conifer forests.

Canary Island Pine
(*Pinus canariensis*)

Needles ~ in 3's, 9 to 12 inches long, light gray-green and glossy when young, grow in dense, drooping tufts on ends of branchlets.

Cones ~ 4 to 9 inches long; pendulous; ovoid-cylindric; light brown.

Bark ~ scaly and irregulary furrowed; reddish brown on older trees.

Description ~ grows to 100 feet, 3 feet in diameter, has a narrow, pyramidal crown and slender, spreading branches with drooping branchlets. Yellow shoots distinguish it from all other three leafed pines.

Range ~ Southern California; native to the Canary Islands.

Canary Island Pine

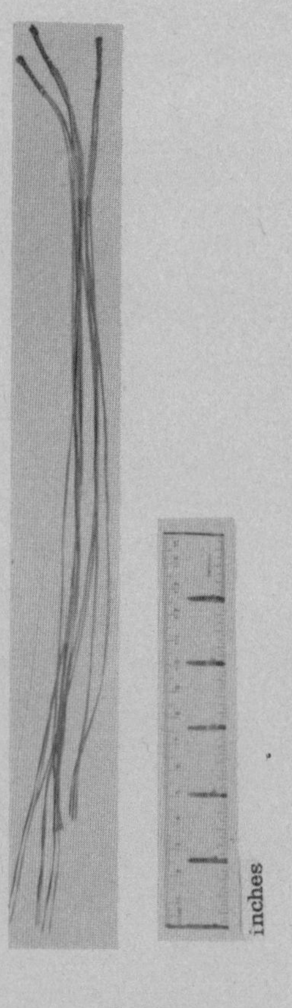

Coulter Pine
(*Pinus coulteri*)

"Big-cone Pine", "Pitch Pine".

Needles ~ 3's, 5 to 12 inches long, stout, stiff, light gray-green with sharp points; form spreading tufts at ends of branches.

Cones ~ 9 to 14 inches long, 5 to 8 inches wide, 4 to 8 pounds (heaviest cone); egg shaped; light yellow brown; scales are large and curve down and out to form hook-like projections with sharp points that resemble birds. Cones on tree 3 to 4 years.

Bark ~ dark gray to blackish; irregular network of deeply furrowed scaly ridges.

Description ~ 35 to 80 feet tall, 1 to 2½ feet in diameter; short trunked with open, wide-spreading irregular crown and long, thick lower branches.

Range ~ 3000 to 6000 feet on dry, rocky slopes from Mt. Diablo (northeast of San Francisco) to Lower California. Most abundant in San Jacinto and San Bernardino ranges.

Coulter Pine

Digger Pine
(*Pinus sabiniana*)

"Nut Pine," "Gray Pine"

Needles ~ in 3's, 7 to 13½ inches long, grayish-green; droop in curves from ends of branches.

Cones ~ 6 to 10 inches long, up to 4 pounds; oblong; light chocolate brown; scales drawn out into a stout, sharp claw. Nut-like seeds are in pockets at the base of each cone scale.

Bark ~ dark gray or brown with large scales that are deeply and irregularly furrowed.

Description ~ 40 to 80 feet tall, 2 to 4 feet in diameter; solitary, open crowned with airy, spreading foliage; not a good shade tree; crooked, forking trunk and branches.

Range ~ below 5,000 feet on the dry slopes and ridges of the California foothills boardering the Central Valley.

Digger Pine

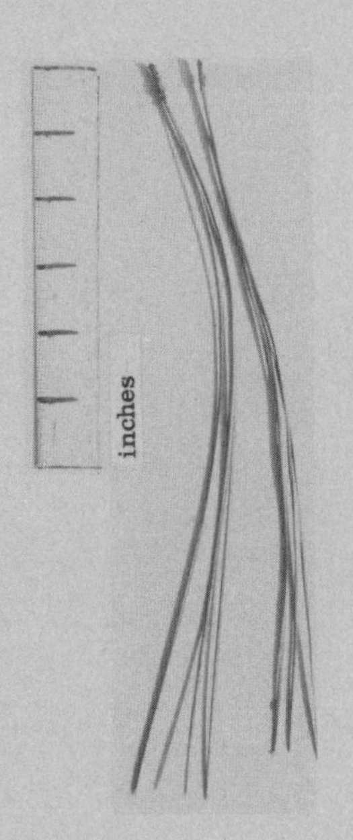

Jeffrey Pine
(<u>Pinus</u> <u>jeffreyi</u>)
"Western Yellow Pine," "Bull Pine"

Needles ~ in 3's (some in 2's and 3's), 5 to 11 inches long; stout, stiff, dull blue/gray green; often twisted.

Cones ~ 5 to 10 inches long, 5 inches wide, conical or egg shaped. Scales are thick and firm and the prickles point down.

Bark ~ vanilla-like odor in furrows, reddish/purplish brown on older trees, dark brown to black on young trees; peels in irregular plates with no yellow underneath.

Description ~ 60 to 180 feet tall, 3 to 4 feet in diameter; thick, straight trunk, big limbs and a spreading crown. Similar to and hybridizes with Ponderosa.

Range ~ 5,500 to 9000 feet from Southern Oregon to Lower California.

Jeffrey Pine

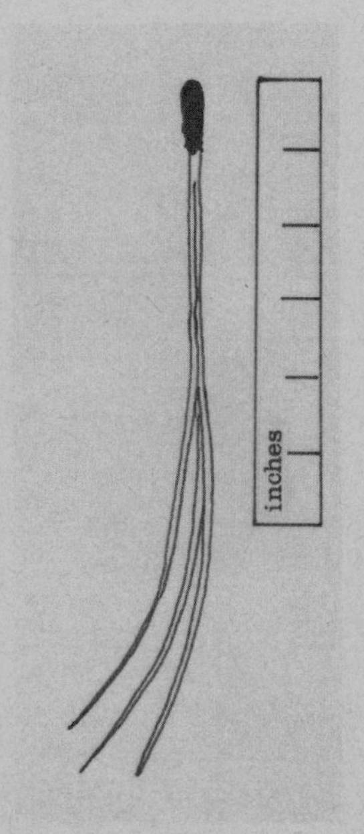

Montezuma Pine
(Pinus montezumae)

"Mexican Pine"

Needles ~ in 5's, to 15 inches or more in length; bluish-green; drooping.

Cones ~ 10 inches long; vary in size and shape; dull yellow to reddish to dark brown in color.

Description ~ 70 to 100 feet tall; rounded and spreading.

Range ~ 4,000 to 12,000 feet; Mexico to Guatemala, some cultivated in Southern California.

There are several P. montezumae types of pines with long needles and some hybridize with P. montezumae.

Montezuma Pine

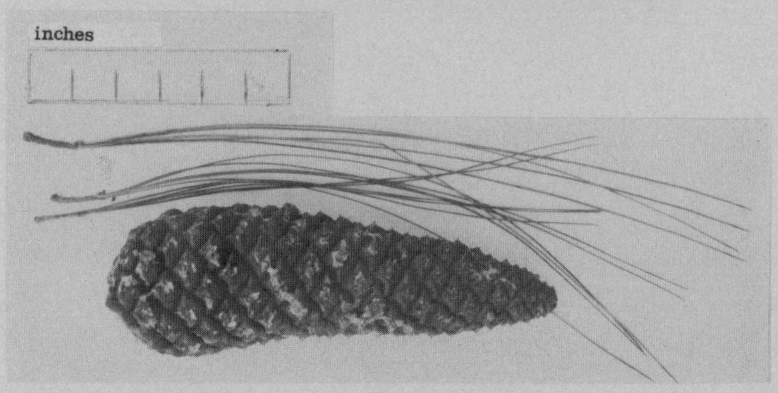

Ponderosa Pine
(Pinus ponderosa)

"Western Yellow Pine," "Silver Pine"

Needles ~ in 3's (some 2 to 5), 5 to 10 inches long, green to dark yellow-green, form tassels on the upturning branch ends.

Cones ~ 2¾ to 6 inches long, 2½ inches wide, oval-cylindric, reddish brown; scales have a short prickle at the tip that points outward.

Bark ~ orange/yellow brown on older trees, dark reddish brown to nearly black on young trees; picture puzzle-like plates peel off easily (yellow under bark).

Description ~ 45 to 230 feet tall, 3 to 6 feet in diameter; tall and symmetrical; on older trees, about ½ of trunk is branchless; hybridizes with Jeffrey Pine making identification difficult. Some live to 600 years.

Range ~ 2000 to 9000 feet in western states from S. British Columbia to N. Mexico.

Ponderosa Pine

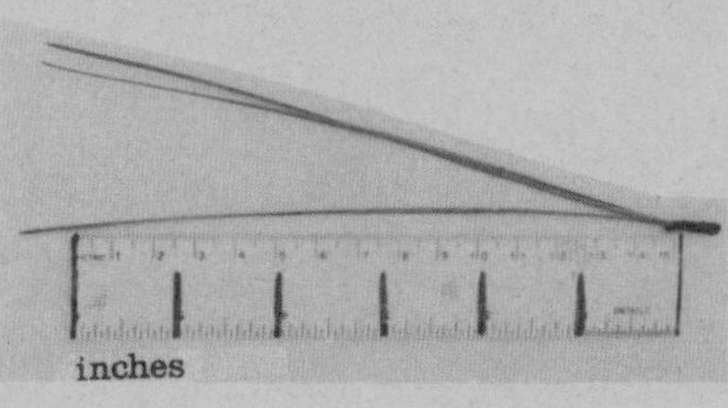

Torrey Pine
(Pinus torreyana)

"Del Mar Pine," "Soledad Pine"

Needles ~ in 5's, up to 13 inches long, dark green, sturdy, rigid, sharp pointed; clusters in large tufts at ends of stout branch ends.

Cones ~ 4 to 6 inches long and almost as wide; broadly ovoid; chest-nut or chocolate brown; scales are thick and have a small prickle on the end.

Bark ~ blackish/reddish brown, scaly and deeply and irregulary furrowed.

Description ~ 30 to 50 feet tall, 1 to 2 feet in diameter; in natural setting it is low, spreading and crooked - under cultivation, it is straight with ascending branches and open crown.

Range ~ its natural habitat is the Torrey Pines Reserve, a small area north of San Diego and on Santa Rosa Island.

Torrey Pine

~Eastern North American Pines~

Loblolly Pine
(*Pinus taeda*)

Needles ~ in 3's, 6 to 9 inches long; slender; yellow green.

Cones ~ 2½ to 6 inches long; oblong; dull, pale, red-brown; scales are thin with a stout, sharp spine.

Bark ~ thin, scaly and nearly black on young trees; bright red-brown and scaly plated on older trees.

Description ~ 90 to 150 feet tall, 2 to 3 feet in diameter; compact, round topped crown of branches on older trees.

Range ~ New Jersey to Florida and Texas.

Loblolly Pine

inches

Longleaf Pine
(*Pinus palustris*)

Needles ~ in 3's, 8 to 18 inches long; slender, flexible; bright green.

Cones ~ 6 to 10 inches long, 3½ inches wide; ovoid-cylindric; red brown with an incurved prickle.

Bark ~ orange-brown with rough, scaly plates.

Description ~ 80 to 120 feet tall, 2 to 3 feet in diameter; open headed with a straight trunk; live up to 300 years.

Range ~ Virginia to Florida and Mississippi.

Longleaf Pine

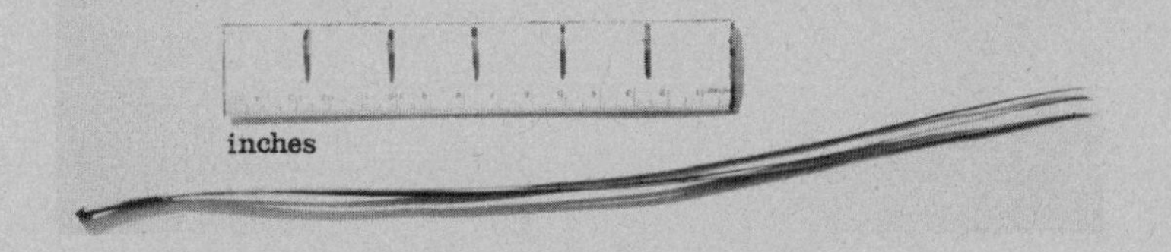

Slash Pine
(*Pinus elliottii*)

Needles ~ in 2's and 3's, 8 to 12 inches long; stout; glossy, dark green.

Cones ~ 2½ to 6 inches long; ovoid; chocolate brown; small, sharp spines.

Bark ~ orange to purple-brown; plated.

Description ~ 80 to 100 feet tall, 2 to 3 feet in diameter; long trunk with dense, rounded crown.

Range ~ Florida and East Coast; principal pine of Central America.

Slash Pine

Young tree

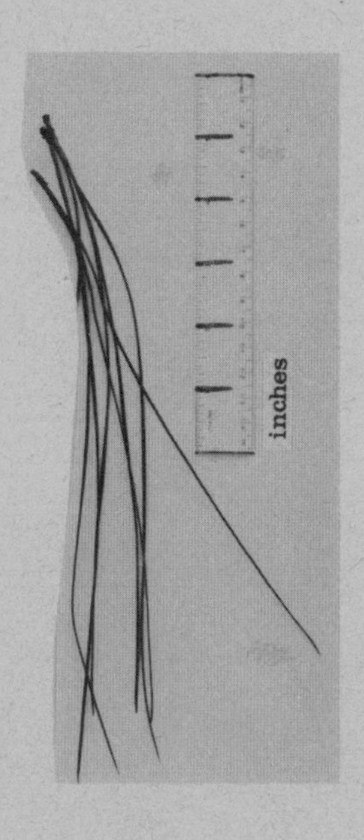

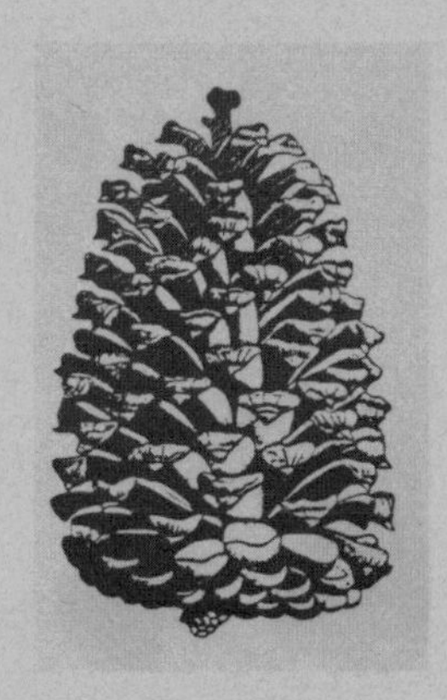

Some usable trees in other countries ~

Benguet Pine (*Pinus insularis*)

Needles ~ in 3's, 9 inches long.

Cones ~ 4 inches long; prickly.

Range ~ Phillippine Islands to Burma and Southern China.

Chir Pine (*Pinus roxburghii*)

Needles ~ in 3's, 8 to 12 inches long; pale green.

Cones ~ conic-ovate, 4 to 7 inches long.

Description ~ up to 180 feet tall; symmetrical head; similar to Canary Island Pine.

Range ~ Himalayas; cultivated in California.

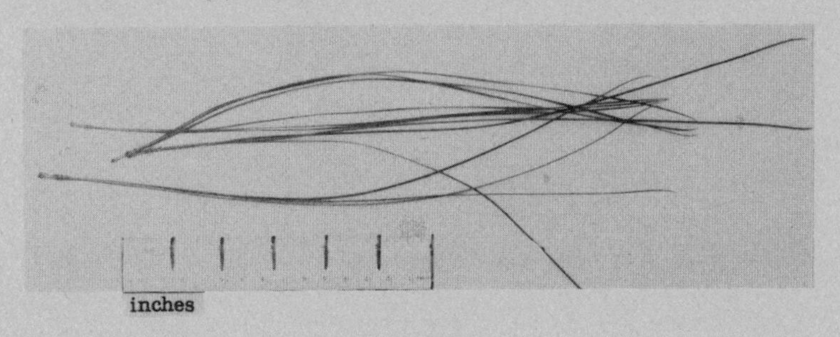

Guatemala Pine (Pinus pseudostrobus)

inches

Needles ~ in 5's, about 16 inches long; beautiful brown when dry; sheath end smaller and more delicate than the Montezuma.

Range ~ Mexico and Central America.

Telecote or Mexican Yellow Pine (Pinus patula)

Needles ~ in 3's, up to 12 inches long; bright grassy-green; drooping.

Cones ~ pale brown

Description ~ spreading leaf pine; conical with upturned branches.

inches

Range ~ Mexico, California.

bibliography

12

PINE NEEDLE BASKETRY
~ BIBLIOGRAPHY ~

Day, Greg. South Carolina Low Country Coil Baskets. (pamphlet). South Carolina: South Carolina Arts Commission, 1977.

Fisher, Kay. Pine Needles to Baskets and Other Things. Camino, California: Kay Fisher publisher, 1983.

Gettys, Marshall (editor). Basketry of Southeastern Indians. Oklahoma: Museum of the Red River, 1984.

Jackson, Nancy. Gullah Baskets. California: unpublished manuscript, 1982.

Jolley, Ginger. How to Weave a Pine Needle Basket. San Bernardino, California: Crown Printers, 1985.

Land, Marie. The Art of Pine Needle Basketry. Lilburn, Georgia: Corner Cupboard Crafts, Inc., 1978.

Loffborough, M. and Cain, E. Pine Needle Basketry. New York: Century House Pub. Co., Inc., 1978. Reprint of 1913 & 1963 editions.

Mc Farland, Jeannie. Pine Needle Raffia Basketry. Redmond, Oregon: Midstate Printing Inc., 1978.

Mc Farland, Jeannie. Advanced Pattern Book For Pine Needle Raffia Basketry. Redmond, Oregon: Midstate Printing Inc., 1980.

Meilach, Dona Z and Menagh, Dee. Basketry Today With Materials From Nature.

New York: Crown Publishers, Inc., 1979.

Millikin, Lenna Leohr. *Pine Needle Baskets.* Seattle, Washington: Facsimile Reproduction, 1973. Reprint of 1920 edition.

Stillwell, Alexandra. *The Technique of Teneriffe Lace.* Watertown, Mass.: Charles T. Branford Co., 1980.

Walsh, Veronica J. *The Book of Pine Needle Craft.* Tampa, Florida: Hillsboro, Printing, 1961, 1970, 1977. Book one revised.

Washington, Misti. "Pine Needle Basketry". *Shuttle, Spindle and Dyepot.* Vol, XVI, No. 4, Issue 64 (Fall 1985), p. 46-51.

PINE TREE
~ BIBLIOGRAPHY ~

Arno, Stephen F.. Discovering Sierra Trees. California: Yosemite Natural History Association and Sequoia Natural History Association, 1973.

Brown, Vinson and Livezey, Robert. The Sierra Nevadan Wildlife Region. Naturegraph, Co, 1962.

Collins, Barbara J. Key to Trees and Wildflowers of the Mountains of Southern California. Thousand Oaks, California. California Lutheran College, 1974.

Gerstenberg, R.H. Common Trees and Shrubs of the Southern Sierra Nevada. Reedley, California: Kings River College, 1983.

Lewis, Mildred Bell. Interesting California Trees of Forest, Desert and City. Pasadena, California: Pacific Book and Printing, 1983.

Little, Elbert L. The Audubon Society Field Guide to North American Trees, Western Region. New York: Knopf, 1980.

Muir, John. The Coniferous Forests and Big Trees of the Sierra Nevada. Golden, Colorado: Outbooks, 1980. Reprint of 1878 and 1881 edition.

Peterson, Russell. The Pine Tree Book. New York: Brandywine Press, Inc., 1980.

This book is available through:

Judy Mulford
2098 Mandeville Canyon Road
Los Angeles, California, 90049